CHARMING
HOTELS & RESORTS

Charm, luxury and *good taste* are not always found together. But this is the combination we aim to capture as we re-build our list, a network of delightful hotels and resorts in the *Charming Hotels'* spiritual home of Italy, and in the wide world beyond.

More than just a listing of hotels, this directory is packed with information and maps to help you plan your trip. *Study* it well, and be sure to *enjoy* the journey.

"The world is a book, and those who do not travel read only one page" said Augustine of Hippo over 1,500 years ago.

Keep travelling, and don't hesitate to *contact us* for advice or to make your reservation.

Thomas Howells
Chairman
International Hotel Network Limited

WWW.CHARMINGHOTELS.COM
+39 06 977 4591

Charming Hotels & Resorts of Italy and beyond: Directory 2010

Published by International Hotel Network Limited,
27 John Street, London WC1N 2BX

Text © 2010 International Hotel Network Limited
and Blue Guides Limited

Produced for International Hotel Network Limited
by Blue Guides Limited, a Somerset Books company.
Photo research and design: Hadley Kincade; Text: Judy Tither based on Blue Guides with permission; Hotels coordinator: Elisabeth Meinertzhagen;
Maps © Blue Guides and Dimap Bt; Layout: Éva Miklya;
Pre-press: HVG Studio. Printed in Italy by Marchesi.

All rights reserved. No part of this publication may be reproduced or used by any means without the permission of the publisher.

ISBN 978-1-905-131-43-3

A CIP catalogue record of this book is available from the British Library.

Distributed in the United States of America, Canada, Australia and New Zealand by WW Norton & Company, Inc.
500 Fifth Avenue, New York, NY 10110.

While the publisher has made reasonable efforts to ensure the accuracy of the information herein contained, it cannot accept responsibility or liability for information supplied by hotels to the publisher. Readers should be aware that conditions and prices can change without notice.

Other copyright information and photo credits are given on p. 182, which forms a part of this copyright page.

RESERVATIONS

To make a reservation:

1. *Speak* to us: staff in our Rome office know our properties and can advise on the facilities offered. On the telephone you will be offered the best Internet rate that we have, so it costs you no more than booking online:

+39 06 977 4591
(during office hours)

2. *Book online:* our website has information and photo galleries on all our hotels, guaranteed best rates and immediate online availability and bookings for most properties:

www.charminghotels.com

3. *Email us:*

reservations@charminghotels.com

4. Contact your *Travel Agent.*

5. *Travel Agents* should call +39 06 977 4591 or write to reservtions@charminghotels.com for an immediate response, or book using the GDS code CU.

6. Our *Mailing Addresses:*

Head office:	Italian branch:
International Hotel Network Limited	Charming Hotels & Resorts
27 John Street	Piazza S. Salvatore in Lauro, 13
London WC1N 2BX	00186 Rome

WWW.CHARMINGHOTELS.COM
+39 06 977 4591

INTRODUCTION

Hotels are affiliated to the Charming Hotels & Resorts network to present their unique values to discerning travellers: values of a sense of place, a warmth of welcome, and of luxury combined with charm.

This directory presents our hotels for 2010, along with information and clear maps to help you plan your trip.

Charming Hotels was founded in 1987 by TCL SpA, an Italian luxury hospitality group. This is the first annual directory from the network's new owners, International Hotel Network Limited of London, part of the Blue Guides group. Launched in 1918, Blue Guides has long been a leading publisher of practical and cultural guide books, particularly to Italy.

Our Rome office exists to inform our guests and support our hotels and travel professionals throughout the world. Please contact us with any questions:

Alastair Graham, Managing Director
managingdirector@charminghotels.com

Ornella Bernini, Sales Manager
sales@charminghotels.com

Elisabeth Meinertzhagen, Marketing Manager
marketing@chaminghotels.com

Irene Casola, Affiliations Manager
affiliations@chaminghotels.com

Cristina Cozma, Distribution Manager
distribution@chaminghotels.com

For advice and reservations:
Charming Hotels (GDS code CU)
reservations@charminghotels.com

WWW.CHARMINGHOTELS.COM
+39 06 977 4591

CONTENTS

Welcome	1
Reservations	3
Introduction	4
Key	7
Charming Hotels & Resorts	9
Amenities	173
Spa services	174
Fitness facilities	175
Golf	176
Tennis	177
Children's activities	178
Meeting facilities	179
GDS codes	180

ITALY...

CAMPANIA	10
Capri	12
Hotel La Floridiana	16
Ischia	18
Hotel Miramare e Castello	22
Sorrento	24
La Tonnarella	28
EMILIA ROMAGNA	30
Rimini	32
National Hotel	36
LAZIO	38
Rome	40
Hotel d'Inghilterra	46
Hotel Homs	48
Residenza di Ripetta	50
Hotel Sole al Pantheon	52
Residenza Torre Colonna	54
Hotel Villa Morgagni	56
LOMBARDY	58
Lake Garda	60
Hotel Villa del Sogno	64
PUGLIA	66
Castelanetta Marina	68
Alborea Eco Lodge	72
Grand Hotel Kalidria	74
SARDINIA	76
Cala Capra	78
Hotel Capo d'Orso Thalasso & Spa	82
Santa Teresa Gallura	84
Valle dell'Erica Resort Thalasso & Spa	88
SICILY	90
Favignana	92
Cave Bianche Hotel	96
TUSCANY	98
Florence	100
Hotel Helvetia & Bristol	106
Villa Stanley	108
Siena	110
Grand Hotel Continental	116

CONTENTS

VENETO 118
Venice 120
Hotel Excelsior 126
Hotel Villa Franceschi 128
Asolo 130
Hotel Villa Cipriani 134

Vicenza 136
Hotel Villa Michelangelo 140
Cortina d'Ampezzo 142
Park Hotel Faloria 146

...AND BEYOND

SWITZERLAND
Geneva 148
Hotel Bristol 154

TURKEY
Istanbul 156
Sirkeci Konak 162

JAPAN
Kyoto 164
Hotel Granvia Kyoto 170

WWW.CHARMINGHOTELS.COM
+39 06 977 4591

KEY

Air conditioned	Outdoor dining
Beach nearby	Outdoor swimming pool
Beauty centre	Outstanding atmosphere
Children's facilities	Outstanding cuisine
Disabled access	Panoramic view
Fitness centre	Parking facilities (garage)
Garden/park	Parking facilities (open air)
Golf course	Pets allowed
Hairdresser	Piano-bar/dancing
Historic building	Place of art and culture
Indoor dining	Private beach
Indoor swimming pool	Shops
In-room business facilities	Spa
Jacket and tie required	Tennis court
Jacuzzi	Wellness Centre
Massages	Yachting facilities
No-smoking rooms	

WWW.CHARMINGHOTELS.COM
+39 06 977 4591

Italy

CHARMING HOTELS & RESORTS

ITALY HOTELS

Location	Region	Page
● Asolo	Veneto	130
● Cala Capra	Sardinia	78
● Capri	Campania	12
● Castellaneta Marina	Puglia	68
● Cortina d'Ampezzo	Veneto	142
● Favignana	Sicily	92
● Florence & Sesto Fiorentino	Tuscany	100
● Gardone Riviera & Lake Garda	Lombardy	60
● Ischia	Campania	18
● Rimini	Emilia Romagna	32
● Rome	Lazio	40
● Santa Teresa Gallura	Sardinia	84
● Siena	Tuscany	110
● Sorrento	Campania	24
● Venice & Mira	Veneto	120
● Vicenza & Arcugnano	Veneto	136

Charming Hotels organized by city or nearest town (see map opposite).

REST OF WORLD HOTELS

City	Country	Page
● Geneva	Switzerland	148
● Istanbul	Turkey	156
● Kyoto	Japan	164

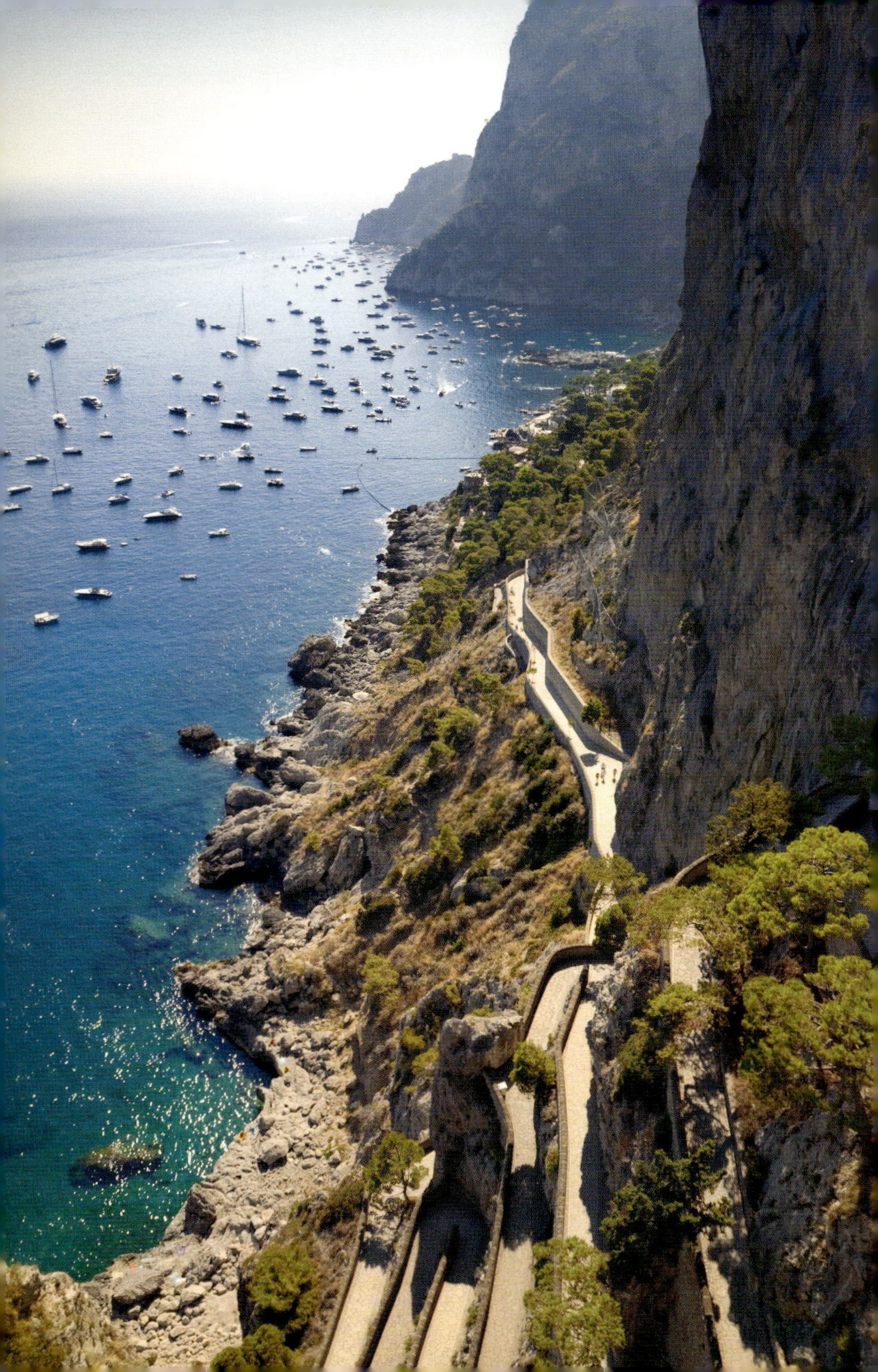

① **HOTEL LA FLORIDIANA** p.16
② **HOTEL MIRAMARE E CASTELLO** p.22
③ **LA TONNARELLA** p.28

Campania
BAY OF NAPLES

The Romans called it Campania Felix, 'the Happy Land', on account of its beauty and fertility. Important places to visit are Naples, Pompeii, the Amalfi Coast with its precipitously built towns and villages, the island of Capri and the beautifully preserved temples at Paestum.

CAPRI, with its almost constant sunshine, crystal clear air and luscious flora, is a captivating place at any time of the year. An extension of the Sorrentine peninsula, it is only 6km long and 3km wide, and is just 5km from the tip of the mainland. Mountainous and rocky, the cliffs plunge directly into the sea and the 17km coastline is pierced with secret coves and grottoes, the most famous being the Grotta Azzurra or Blue Grotto. The two main centres are the sophisticated town of Capri and the smaller village of Anacapri to the west. Traffic on the island is limited to small buses and a few taxis, which undoubtedly does much to enhance its charm.

Capri town sits 142m above sea-level between the island's highest point, Monte Solaro, and Punta del Capo, the eastern tip. From the main harbour, Marina Grande, steep pathways and a funicular make the ascent to the town's central square, Piazza Umberto Primo—or the Piazzetta, as it is known to the local Capresi. This lively square, always bustling with people, is an ideal spot to sit at one of the many cafés, relax over a drink and watch the world swirl around you; the evening's ritual of the *passeggiata* is an especially engrossing parade of the locals in their finery, wanting to see and to be seen. Here you will also find the best restaurants, while the streets off the square, particularly Via Vittorio Emanuele and Via Camerelle, are the best for exclusive designer shops. Away from the main square, the Certosa di San Giacomo is a romantically derelict Carthusian monastery, a cool place to wander in and relax.

Capri

HISTORY Beguiling visitors to its dramatic shores for over 2,000 years, it was Emperor Tiberius who turned Capri into a playboy's paradise, a description which still holds true. Long a sleepy fishing village, fought over during the Napoleonic Wars, by the middle of the 19th century it had become an exclusive haven for artists, writers and intellectuals from Europe and beyond.

CULTURE Perfume has been produced on Capri for centuries. Manufacture was started in 1380 by the prior of the Certosa and perfumes are still created using the finest natural ingredients. Visit the Carthusia Profumeria at Viale Parco Augusto 2a.

FOOD It's only natural that the sea provides the foundation of Caprese cuisine; simple grilled lobster and other shell-fish feature on most menus. Stuffed calamari, originally a peasant dish, is now a sophisticated classic, accompanied by the local crisp white wine. Sauces use locally-grown tomatoes and cheese. *Torta Caprese* is a delicious chocolate and almond cake.

EVENTS 14th May: feast day of the island's patron saint, San Costanzo. The saint's image is paraded through the streets.
25–29th May: Rolex Sailing Week.
12th September: Festa di Santa Maria della Libera, procession through the streets of Marina Grande. Evening concert concludes with a midnight fireworks display.

TRANSPORTATION
Ferries from Naples, Sorrento, Ischia: April–Oct. Hydrofoil from Naples, Sorrento, Ischia: April–Oct, Positano and Amalfi: www.capritourism.com. No private cars; buses and taxis from Marina Grande to Piazza Umberto Primo, Marina Piccola and Anacapri. Funicular from Marina Grande to Piazza Umberto Primo leaves every 15mins.

POPULATION: 12,000
AREA CODE: + 39 081
TOURIST OFFICE: + 39 081 837 5308
www.capritourism.com

Hotel La Floridiana
Via Campo di Teste, 16
80073 Capri
www.charminghotels.com/
hotellafloridiana

General Manager
Mrs Lucia Esposito

Open from
7th March to 3rd November

Rooms & Facilities
32 Rooms and suites
Bar and restaurant
Swimming pool
(opening in 2010)
Spa services
(corner shiatsu massage)

Rates
Double from €150 to 380
Junior Suite from €280 to 440
Suite from €450 to 820
VAT, breakfast & service
charge included

Credit Cards
Visa, Mastercard, American
Express, Diners

Airport
Naples Capodichino (NAP)
30 km/18 miles

Train Station
Naples Central
25 km/15 miles

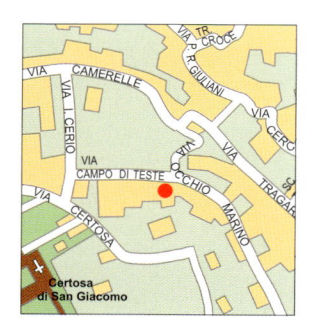

WWW.CHARMINGHOTELS.COM
+39 06 977 4591

HOTEL LA FLORIDIANA

This small, modern, Mediterranean-style hotel is close to the centre of Capri town, near Via Camerelle, the town's main shopping street, the busy Piazzetta with its shops and cafés, and the evocative deserted Carthusian monastery, the Certosa di San Giacomo.

Surrounded by cooling pine trees, the hotel faces south overlooking the bay towards the Marina Piccola and the Faraglioni rocks. The 36 generously-sized guest rooms and suites are elegant and brightly decorated, each in its own individual distinctive style, with delicately painted pieces of furniture and majolica-tiled floors. Some rooms have balconies or terraces with marvellous sea views, while others have views across the fragrant gardens.

Simona Paone
Owner

An extensive breakfast with a wide choice of breads, cereals and meats, is served on the terrace, from which there are breathtaking views over the pine woods to the sea. The comfortable wine bar serves light meals and drinks throughout the day, with a more substantial and sophisticated menu in the evenings.

From the hotel there are stunning walks down the hillside to the beach and to the nearby Gardens of Augustus.

ISCHIA lies in the Tyrrhenian Sea and is the largest island in the Bay of Naples. This mountainous, volcanic island is made up of craters and lava beds. The highest point is Monte Epomeo (788m), an extinct volcano, and it is this volcanic activity which helped to create Ischia's greatest attraction, its 29 spas, 67 fumaroles and103 hot springs. With its mild climate and fertile volcanic soil, Ischia is lush and verdant, attractive to artists, walkers and anyone wanting to relax in peaceful natural surroundings.

Divided into six *comuni*, the oldest part is Ischia Ponte, now a chic area with art galleries and interesting little artisans' shops, which grew up around the picturesque Castello Aragonese, which sits on a rocky islet. There has been a fortification here since 474 BC but it was Alfonso of Aragon who refortified it in 1438. This was where the islanders would seek refuge from pirate raids; it also housed the cathedral, a convent and churches, as well as the barracks.

Further along the sandy coast is Ischia Porto, a bustling modern area around the harbour, developed since the 18th century when the port was created. It has a relaxed atmosphere with numerous restaurants, cafés and bars.

Further along, Casamicciola Terme was where the first of the island's many thermal spas were first exploited by the discerning travellers of the 18th and 19th centuries. Away from the coast, it is possible to climb Monte Epomeo, which last erupted in 1301.

Ischia

History Ischia was home to the legendary giant Typhoeus, who challenged Jupiter's thunderbolts with earthquakes and volcanoes, Augustus always preferred Capri, and in the Middle Ages it was sacked by pirates. Eventually its fortunes soared as spas and thermal treatments became fashionable in the 18th and 19th centuries.

Culture Ischia's greatest asset is its thermal spas, the therapeutic effects of which have been known since Roman times. The art of straw-weaving has almost died out but there is a thriving handicraft industry producing hand-painted majolica tiles and terracotta pottery.

Food Among the hearty peasant dishes is wild rabbit stewed in a terracotta pot with tomatoes, spices and wine. Snails are harvested from the stone walls and stewed with wine and garlic.

Events Easter: parades and re-enactment of Christ's Passion.
26th July: festival of Sant'Anna, with decorated floats in the bay and fireworks from Castello Aragonese.
26th August: feast of Sant'Alessandro, Ischia Porto, parade of local costume.

Transportation
Daily ferries from Naples, Pozzuoli, Procida and Capri. Daily hydrofoil services from Naples, Procida and Capri, www.campaniatrasporti.com. The island is closed to cars but buses leave from Ischia Porto and make a circuit of the island.

Population: 60,000
Area code: +39 081
Tourist office: +39 081 507 4211
www.infoischiaprodica.it

Hotel & Fine Restaurant Miramare e Castello

Via Pontano, 5
80077 Ischia, Naples
www.charminghotels.com/miramarecastello

General Manager
Mr Giovanni Monti

Open
23rd April to 10th October

Rooms & Facilities
41 Rooms and suites
Health and beauty programs
Private beach
Solarium with jacuzzi

Rates
Single from €145 to 240
Double from €210 to 520
Suite from €450 to 640
VAT, breakfast & service charge included

Dining
Miramare Restaurant on the beach

Meeting Rooms: 1
Capacity: 30 max
Package rates: on request

Credit Cards
Visa, MasterCard, American Express, Diners

Airport
Naples Capodichino (NAP)
29 km/18 miles

WWW.CHARMINGHOTELS.COM
+39 06 977 4591

Hotel Miramare e Castello

Positioned above its own private beach in the picturesque village of Ischia Ponte, the island's historic main town, Miramare e Castello offers timeless elegance and luxury.

Views from the hotel take in the Castello Aragonese, the Bay of Naples, the Sorrentine peninsula and the island of Capri.

Giovanni Monti
General Manager

The spacious rooms either look out over Monte Epomeo, the highest point on the island, or across the bay towards the mainland. All rooms are light and airy, brightly painted in pastel shades and have tiled bathrooms and modern furnishings.

An extensive breakfast buffet is served on the roof terrace, while light lunches and dinner are served in the sea-front restaurant, the Miramare, or on a floating deck over the water. Using only the finest local ingredients, the menu features a wide choice of local-style dishes as well as international specialities, all beautifully prepared and presented.

There is also a Technogym fitness centre, a beauty spa offering a variety of treatments including total body massages, sauna and hydro-massage, and two roof-top jacuzzis.

SORRENTO Perched high above the Bay of Naples, with exceptional views of Vesuvius, Naples and Ischia, Sorrento lies in an area of great natural beauty. It is a busy, welcoming place with particularly good road, rail and sea links. Sorrento is an ideal base from which to explore the magnificent Sorrentine peninsula and the Amalfi Coast with its delightful little towns, such as Positano, Amalfi and Ravello, tumbling down to the sea to the west, while to the east the major archaeological sites of Pompeii, Herculanium and Oplontis are only a short train journey away.

Whether it's sitting in Piazza Tasso sipping a cup of coffee while looking over the gorge and out to sea, or wandering the characteristic little lanes, Sorrento is an attractive place to spend your time. What the town may lack in terms of conventional 'sites' is more than made up for in magnificent panoramic views and tranquil secluded corners. The 14th-century church of San Francesco still has a peaceful flower-filled cloister with crisply carved, interlaced arches typical of this area of Campania. Next to the cathedral is a beautiful garden from which there are impressive views across the Bay of Naples.

While there is a small beach at the old port, and some of the hotels have private beaches at the foot of precipitous cliffs, it is the relaxed atmosphere, the splendid views and its proximity to so many other delightful towns and villages which makes Sorrento and its surroundings such a pleasant place to stay.

Sorrento

HISTORY From earliest times Sorrento was a place of leisure; the Romans favoured its climate and its views. Once a short-lived maritime republic, Sorrento was reborn in the 19th century when it became a favourite winter resort for Europeans and Grand Tourists.

CULTURE Intarsia work is a speciality of Sorrento; a museum displays many magnificent examples of this inlaid woodwork. Coral was an important industry in the 15th–18th centuries and there are still example of this craft in many shops and in the coral museum.

FOOD All around the town there are orange and lemon groves and Sorrento is noted for the digestif limoncello. The cuisine of the area is simple and wholesome, fresh fish landed daily at the harbour, with locally-grown tomatoes, courgettes, aubergines and beans.

EVENTS Good Friday: a vivid procession which lasts from dawn to dusk, recalling the Passion of Christ. September: The Incontri Internazionale del Cinema film festival.

TRANSPORTATION
Circumvesuviana Railway, hourly from Naples to Sorrento.
Regular buses from Naples to Sorrento; local (SITA) buses cover the Sorrentine peninsula.
Hydrofoils from Naples to Sorrento, and from Sorrento on to Capri and Ischia. www.campaniatrasporti.it

POPULATION: 17,000
AREA CODE: + 39 081
TOURIST OFFICE: + 39 081 807 4033
www.sorrentotourism.it

La Tonnarella
Via Capo, 31
80067 Sorrento
www.charminghotels.com/hotellatonnerella

General Manager
Mr Giuseppe Gargiulo

Open
1st April to 31st October

Rooms & Facilities
24 Rooms and suites
Private beach
Solarium
Disabled facilities
Parking facilities

Rates
Double Single Use from €102 to 130
Classic Double from €112 to 225
Junior Suite from €240 to 350
Suite from €300 to 400
VAT, breakfast & service charge included

Dining
La Tonnarella Restaurant and Terrace

Credit Cards
Visa, MasterCard, American Express, Eurocard, JCB International

Airport
Naples Capodichino (NAP)
50 km/31 miles

Train Station
Sorrento
1.5 km/1 mile

GDS CHAIN CODE: CU
AMADEUS CU RROLTS
GALILEO CU 79889
SABRE CU 53203
WORLDSPAN CU RROLT

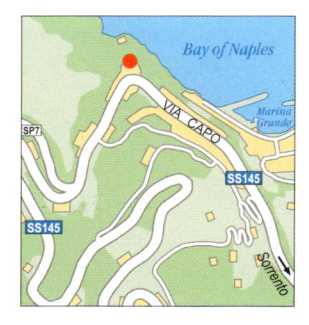

WWW.CHARMINGHOTELS.COM
+39 06 977 4591

LA TONNARELLA

Just a short walk from the bustling centre of Sorrento, this peaceful hotel is perched high on a spur of rock overlooking the Bay of Naples. Named after the typical fishing nets used to catch tuna, La Tonnarella was built as the summer villa of a local family and it has been sensitively converted into this very attractive 24-room hotel, retaining some of the unique architectural details and exquisite ceramic tiles.

Giuseppe Gargiulo
Owner

Offering a choice of accommodation from classic rooms to suites with jacuzzis or hydro-massage pools, many of the rooms have stunning sea views. All are bright and comfortably furnished with traditional polished wood furniture, antiques and hand-painted majolica detailing on the walls and floors.

The restaurant has a panoramic terrace overlooking the bay, with breathtaking views across to Mount Vesuvius. Using the finest local ingredients, including seasonal lobster, shrimps and calamari, the chef creates superb combinations of colour and flavour accompanied by a selection of expertly chosen wines.

An elevator descends a narrow ravine, filled with fragrant wild flowers, to La Tonnarella's private beach, where lunches are served.

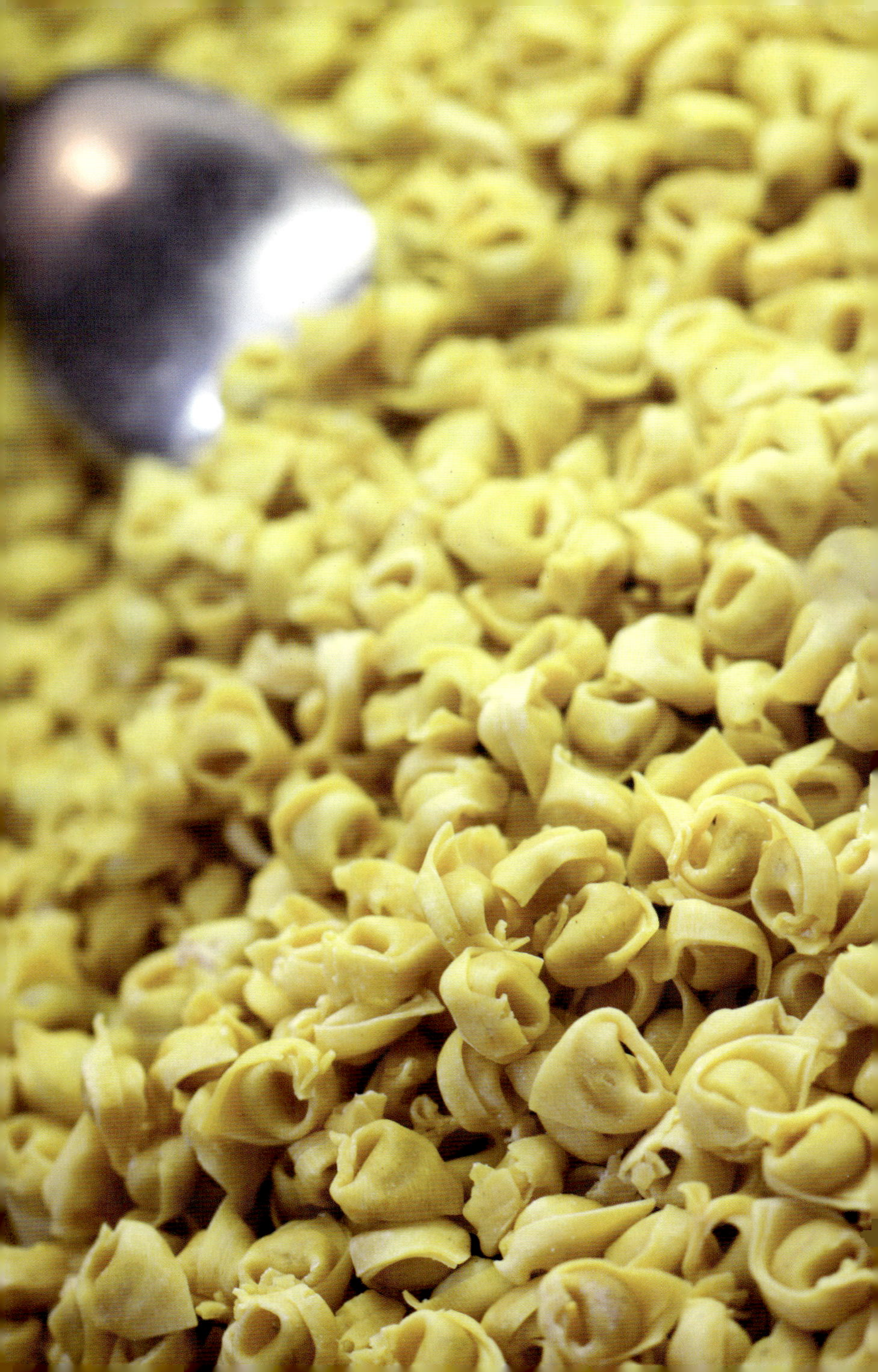

1 NATIONAL HOTEL p.36

Emilia Romagna

Emilia Romagna's name derives from the Via Aemilia, the ancient Roman road that runs through it. In reality the region is two distinct entities. Emilia is the inland part, with Bologna Modena and Parma. Romagna denotes the eastern half with Rimini, Ravenna and Ferrara.

31

RIMINI Famous for its bathing beaches since its 1950s' heyday, Rimini also boasts a historic town centre a kilometre from the seafront.

It remains the epitome of a Mediterranean seaside resort, with its long line of bathing facilities stretching in both directions, and the very latest in seashore services including aerobic gyms, beach libraries and dance floors, as well as green spaces and bars and cafés.

When the sun goes down Rimini's spotlight turns inland to the old centre. Piazza Tre Martiri, the Roman forum in earlier times, is where the locals meet today for a drink and to while away the evening. Foremost among its many ancient buildings is Tempio Malatestiano, one of the most outstanding monuments of the Italian Renaissance. In 1447–48, Sigismondo Malatesta, a brave soldier and daring *condottiere*, commissioned Leon Battista Alberti to transform the 13th-century church of San Francesco into a mausoleum for himself and his third wife, Isotta degli Atti. Sigismondo's arms (an elephant and a rose) and initials (SI) can be seen throughout the building.

There are also splendid Roman remains: the magnificent Arco d'Augusto dates from 27 BC, the amphitheatre from the 2nd century (it could hold 15,000 spectators) and the Ponte d'Augusto e Tiberio has been in use since AD 21.

Rimini

HISTORY The Romans built a colony here in 268 BC, a stronghold against the Gauls. The Malatesta family emerged from papal and imperial infighting as rulers of the city between the 13th and 16th centuries, but a period of decline followed until the first bathing establishments were built in 1843. Since then Rimini has been well-known as a resort.

CULTURE Italian film maestro Federico Fellini was born in Rimini and was undoubtedly influenced by the films he saw at the Cinema Folgor. Episodes from his early life here are said to have inspired many of his films, which combine fantasy with bizarre, surreal images.

FOOD The best food of the region is based on the simplest ingredients: fresh fish, locally-produced cheese, sun-ripened vegetables, flavoured with herbs. A typical snack is a *piadina*, a circle of flat bread, folded in half and filled with cold meat and cheese.

EVENTS June:
International Traditional Jazz and Swing Festival.
2nd July: Pink Night, the Riviera takes on a pink colour, shops, museums open throughout the night, concerts and pink fireworks.
July–August: Amarena and Cinema under the Stars, open-air film festival.
September: Sagra Musicale Malatestiana: classical music festival.

TRANSPORTATION
Federico Fellini airport is 6km south of Rimini. The train station, on Piazzale Cesare Battisti, has fast Eurostar and Intercity services to major cities, as well as local commuter trains. Trolley buses run from Piazza Tre Martiri to the station and to the beach.

POPULATION: 142,000
AREA CODE: + 39 0541
TOURIST OFFICE: + 39 0541 51331
WWW.RIMINITURISMO.IT

National Hotel
Viale A. Vespucci, 42
47900 Rimini
www.charminghotels.com/nationalhotel

General Manager
Mr Pier Luigi Grossi

Open
17th January to
19th December

Rooms & Facilities
99 Rooms and suites
Heated outdoor pool
Modern conference centre
Private spa room

Rates
Single from €55 to 205
Double from €85 to 290
Suite from €155 to 620
VAT, breakfast & service charge included

Dining
Panoramic restaurant

Meeting Rooms: 5
Capacity: 250 max
Package rates: on request

Credit Cards
Visa, American Express, BankAmericard, Diners, MasterCard, CartaSi, JCB

Airports
Bologna Airport (BLQ)
100 km/62 miles
Rimini Airport (RHI)
5 km/3.1 miles

Train Station
Rimini
1.5 km/0.93 miles

GDS CHAIN CODE: CU
AMADEUS CU RMIATI
GALILEO CU 74168
SABRE CU 58738
WORLDSPAN CU NATI

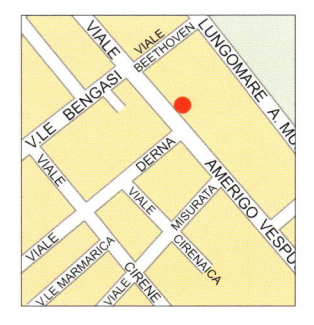

WWW.CHARMINGHOTELS.COM
+39 06 977 4591

NATIONAL HOTEL

The thoroughly modern-looking National Hotel combines the sharpest design elements with tradition, elegance and comfort. Set in the prime location of Marina Centro, the hotel overlooks the beach and is ideally positioned for the town's shops and restaurants. Close by is the historic centre, with one of the most outstanding monuments of the Italian Renaissance, the Tempio Malatestiano.

**Cinzia and Marzia
Front Desk Staff**

private terraces. The Villa dei Gelsomini is a new 12-suite annexe close to the hotel.

The National Hotel has two restaurants, Il Ristorantino, offering a *menu à la grande carte* and the Ristorante Riviera directly on the beach. Both serve international and locally-sourced regional dishes, accompanied by wines from the hotel's well-stocked cellar.

The reception areas are adorned with carefully selected antique furniture and porcelain, a pleasing blend of modern and traditional. The 83 bedrooms are contemporary and tastefully furnished There are 3 roof-top suites with

The amenities include an outdoor swimming pool, jacuzzi, sauna and the Oasi del Benessere, a rooftop wellness centre. The *Ninabella*, the hotel's motor yacht, is available for trips on the Adriatic.

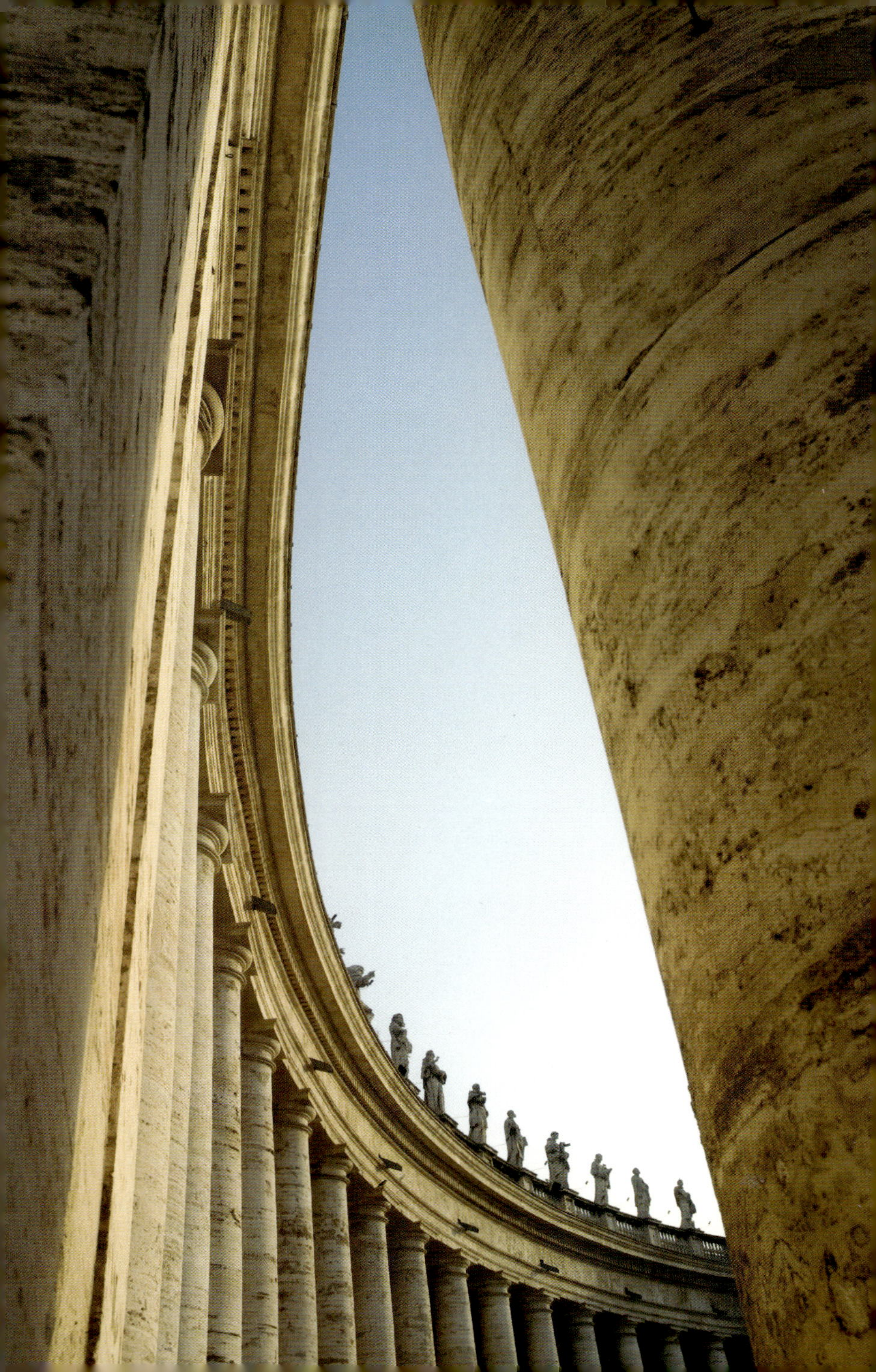

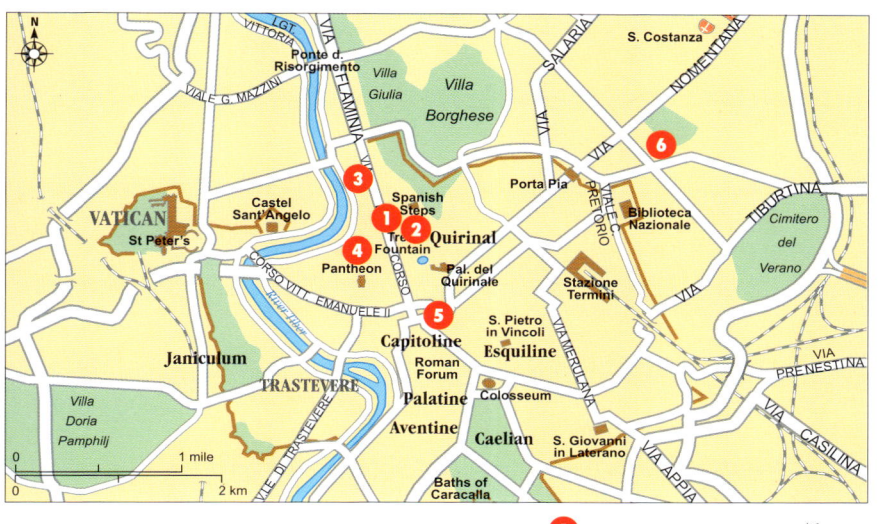

1. Hotel d'Inghilterra p.46
2. Hotel Homs p.48
3. Residenza di Ripetta p.50
4. Hotel Sole al Pantheon p.52
5. Residenza Torre Colonna p.54
6. Hotel Villa Morgagni p.56

Rome

The history of Lazio is both the history of Rome and the history of the Etruscans, the mysterious ancient civilization who occupied this region. Rome is the region's most popular destination; Tivoli and Ostia are ancient Roman sites of great importance.

ROME While the buildings and monuments, which for centuries have drawn pilgrims and travellers to Rome, are familiar and instantly recognised—St Peter's, the Roman Forum, the Colosseum, the Pantheon —they never fail to impress in their grandeur and magnificence. As *Caput Mundi* (Head of the World) Rome's influence extended far beyond the city walls into many spheres of everyday life: law, politics, language, religion, the liberal arts and sciences. The influence of Rome radiated throughout its vast empire and continues to shape our lives today.

Rome is a fascinating kaleidoscope of architectural styles. Though separated by centuries, Imperial temples and baths jostle for space next to splendid Baroque *palazzi* and Renaissance churches; turning a corner will reveal totally unexpected views of an ancient dome or a toga-clad emperor perched on top of a column. The city squares are decorated with splendid fountains, masterpieces of sculpture in themselves, and Egyptian obelisks.

But even with its outstanding art collections, magnificent architecture and some of the most impressive ancient ruins, Rome is so much more than just an open-air museum, it is a thoroughly modern, vibrant, growing city where former warehouses and factories have been converted into modern art galleries, theatres and entertainment venues. Rome is always busy so time spent exploring the quieter streets and the smaller museums is particularly rewarding—you might be the only person visiting a tiny *palazzo*, a church with frescoes by Raphael or a private art collection.

Rome

HISTORY The history of Rome, which is built, as every schoolchild knows, on its seven hills, is a mixture of myth and legend, but with a thread of truth running through it. Early Rome is known to have been a kingdom. In the 6th century BC it became a republic of two main classes: nobles (patricians) and commoners (plebeians). Through masterly conquest by its disciplined armies, it assimilated the peoples it defeated. The huge empire collapsed in 476 and it wasn't until the early 7th century that Rome passed under the guardianship of the popes.

The capital of the empire became the capital of the Church, and Rome began to counterbalance the magnificence of the Byzantine East. The popes allied themselves with the Franks and secured the territory that became the Papal States, which they presided over until 1870.

During the Risorgimento, when republican and nationalist feelings ran high, the pope failed to respond and the city was declared a republic. The pope turned to the French to help him retain his realm. In 1870 the Italian army breached the walls of the city and it was declared capital of the Kingdom of Italy.

Spared during the First World War, Rome was badly affected during the second, both by Allied bombing and by German occupation. After the war, Italy's last king abdicated and Italy declared itself a republic.

Culture Rome has countless museums and galleries with works of art by the world's most accomplished artists, but it is the precocious talent of the archetypal Renaissance man, Michelangelo, which stands above all others. The dome of St Peter's was one of his last works, and it rises above the basilica, an iconic symbol of the city. Inside, the beautiful and sensitive *Pietà* is his earliest commission, made when he arrived in the city in 1497 at the age of 21.

Another prodigious talent lured to Rome, in 1592, was Caravaggio, whose intense emotional realism and masterly handling of light brought heightened drama and realism to his subjects and was to the inspire and shape the Baroque movement.

FOOD Rome manages, more than many capital cities, to preserve its traditional, genuinely local cuisine. A true Roman favourite is the artichoke, cooked in many different ways: *alla giudea*, steamed then fried in olive oil or *alla romana*, stuffed using the stem, flavoured with mint. Another classic is *saltimbocca alla romana*, slices of veal with prosciutto and sage.

EVENTS 5–6 January: Befana (Epiphany) is celebrated at night in Piazza Navona.
Shrove Tuesday: carnival celebrations in streets and *piazze*.
21st April: anniversary of the birth Rome, celebrated on the Capitoline Hill.
First Sunday in June: Festa della Repubblica, military parade in Via dei Fori Imperiali.
23rd–24th June: feast days celebrating St Peter and St Paul, the city's patron saints.
July: Festa di Noantri, traditional festival in the Trastevere district.

Transportation

Rome has two airports Fiumicino (Leonardo da Vinci), 13km southwest and connected to the city by trains and buses, and Ciampino, 26km southeast, with shuttle buses to the city centre.

Rome's main train station is Termini, from which fast trains connect to all other major cities in the country. The best way to get around Central Rome is on foot. For outlying areas there is an efficient public transport system of taxis, buses, trams and metro.

Population:
2,800,000
Area code:
+ 39 06
Tourist office:
+ 39 06 488991
www.romaturismo.com

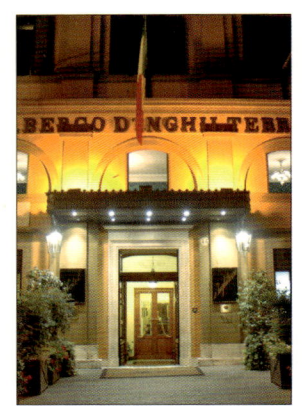

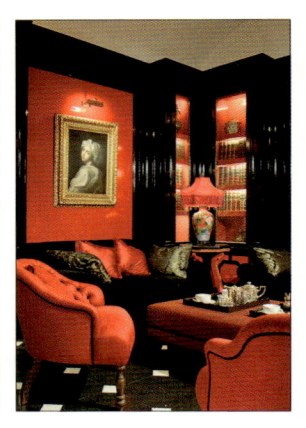

Hotel d'Inghilterra
Via Bocca di Leone, 14
00187 Rome
www.charminghotels.com/
hoteldinghilterra

Hotel Manager
Mr Paolo Ferraro

Open all year

Rooms & Facilities
89 Rooms and suites
Royal Suite with
magnificent terrace or sauna

Rates
Single from €180 to 320
Double from €230 to 580
Suite from €470 to 3500
VAT, breakfast & service
charge not included

Dining
Café Romano Restaurant
Bond Bar

Meeting Rooms: 2
Capacity: 55 max
Package rates: on request

Credit Cards
Visa, MasterCard,
American Express, Diners, JCB

Airports
Rome Fiumicino (FCO)
30 km/19 miles
Rome Ciampino (CIA)
20km/13 miles

Train Station
Rome Termini
2 km/1.2 miles

GDS CHAIN CODE: CU
AMADEUS CU ROMDIN
GALILEO CU 43306
SABRE CU 28263
WORLDSPAN CU 3993

WWW.CHARMINGHOTELS.COM
+39 06 977 4591

Hotel d'Inghilterra

Originally a 17th-century *palazzo* and the guest-house of the Torlonia princes, administrators of the Vatican finances in the 18th and 19th centuries, Hotel d'Inghilterra has been welcoming guests for over 160 years and is one of the most exclusive hotels in Rome. It is situated in a quiet side street in the very heart of the city, close to the Piazza di Spagna and Via Condotti, Rome's smartest and most fashionable shopping area.

Rodolfo Chieroni
Executive Chef

Like the private home it once was, each of the 89 rooms has own distinct style, decorated with the finest period furniture, striking the perfect balance between elegance and comfort. Fifth-floor rooms have terraces with stunning views of Rome's distinctive skyline.

Our restaurant, Café Romano, is an intimate, sophisticated way to experience contemporary Roman cuisine, with seating either inside or on the terrace in the heart of Rome. Open from the early morning, it is ideal for a mid-morning snack, for a light lunch, or for a more sophisticated meal in the evening.

The English-style Bond Bar was named as one of the best in Italy by the *Gambero Rosso* guide. With the intimate atmosphere of a gentleman's club, it is also one of an exclusive group known as Bond Bars, serving a selection of 007's favourite cocktails.

Hotel Homs
Via della Vite, 71/72
00187 Rome
www.charminghotels.com/hotelhoms

General Manager
Mr Gildo Berardini

Open all year

Rooms & Facilities
53 Rooms and suites
Bar and restaurant
Internet connection
Jacuzzi in some rooms

Rates
Single from €100 to 170
Double from €150 to 300
Junior Suite €220 to 450
Deluxe Suite from €250 to 600
Breakfast not included
VAT & service charge included

Credit Cards
Visa, MasterCard, American Express, Diners

Airports
Rome Fiumicino (FCO)
30 km/18 miles
Rome Ciampino (CIA)
20km/13 miles

Train Station
Rome Termini
2 km/1.2 miles

GDS CHAIN CODE: CU
AMADEUS CU ROMH61
GALILEO CU 51370
SABRE CU 64417
WORLDSPAN CU ROM61

WWW.CHARMINGHOTELS.COM
+39 06 977 4591

HOTEL HOMS

The newly redecorated four-star boutique Hotel Homs first opened for business in 1910 and it continues to offer a high standard of comfort. From its ideal location near Piazza di Spagna, many of Rome's most enduring sights, including the Pantheon, the Trevi Fountain and Piazza Navona, are within easy strolling distance, while the fashionable shopping streets of Via Condotti, Via Borgogona and Via del Corso are just around the corner from the hotel.

There are 53 elegant executive rooms with cream-coloured walls and wooden floors, each individually furnished with beautiful fabrics of warm Mediterranean-inspired colours, giving a relaxed, comfortable atmosphere. The suites are on the top floor, again furnished to the highest standards, with private terraces with stunning views of the Roman skyline.

A generous breakfast, with a choice of five menus, is served in the hotel's recently opened Vuda Bar, which overlooks two busy streets, Via della Vite and Via Frattina; a perfect place to watch the world go by. Later in the day, lunch and dinner are served here with choices from the *à la carte* menu, or simple but delicious freshly prepared snacks and sandwiches. The Vuda Bar is also a sophisticated *champagnerie*, offering a wide selection of the best vintages.

Residenza di Ripetta
Via di Ripetta, 231
00186 Rome
www.charminghotels.com/
residenzadiripetta

General Manager
Mr Santino Giusti

Open all year

Rooms & Facilities
69 Rooms and suites
Meeting rooms
Restaurant and bar
Reserved parking
Air conditioning
In-room safe
Kitchenette (in apartments)
Roof garden in spring and summer
Inner garden

Rates
On request

Meeting Rooms: 6
Capacity: 220 max
Package rates: on request

Credit Cards
Visa, MasterCard, American Express, Diners, Maestro Card

Airports
Rome Fiumicino (FCO)
30 km/18 miles
Rome Ciampino (CIA)
20km/13 miles

Train Station
Rome Termini
2.3 km/1.4 miles

GDS CHAIN CODE: CU
AMADEUS CU ROMRRS
GALILEO CU 73423
SABRE CU 7573
WORLDSPAN CU ROMRR

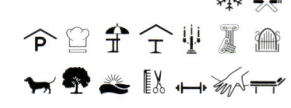

WWW.CHARMINGHOTELS.COM
+39 06 977 4591

RESIDENZA DI RIPETTA

Lying in the historic centre of Rome, between Piazza del Popolo and the Spanish Steps, Residenza di Ripetta is a former 17th-century convent with sober and essential features ideally suited for a full experience of the charm of the Italian capital and comfortable enjoyment of its culture and gastronomy.

Beside ancient frescoes and fascinating sculptures, reminders of Residenza di Ripetta's glorious past, a remarkable collection of contemporary art can be admired, including works by the famous artists Pomodoro and Sinisca.

The 69 suites and apartments are intimate and welcoming, variously sized but all with high ceilings and quiet views, making this hotel the ideal choice both for short and long stays.

The wonderful Roof Garden overlooking the city's rooftops and the quiet Inner Garden are the perfect places to relax while enjoying a cocktail or a coffee.

The well known Meeting Centre comprises 6 meeting rooms. The largest, the Bernini Meeting Room, a former church oratory, can accommodate more than 200 people. These versatile and stylish meeting rooms are ideal for any kind of event.

Santino Giusti
General Manager

Hotel Sole al Pantheon

Piazza della Rotonda, 63
00186 Rome
www.charminghotels.com/hotelsolealpantheon

General Manager
Mr Maurizio Taliano

Open all year

Rooms & Facilities
33 Rooms and suites
Centrally located
In-room business facilities
WI-FI access in common areas

Rates
Single from €140 to 330
Double from €180 to 450
Junior Suite from €240 to 630
Suite Annexe from €280 to 730
VAT, Buffet breakfast & service charge included

Dining
Il Montone Soft Bar
Garden Patio

Credit Cards
Visa, MasterCard, American Express, Diners

Airports
Rome Fiumicino (FCO)
30 km/18 miles
Rome Ciampino (CIA)
20km/13 miles

Train Station
Rome Termini
3 km/1.8 miles

GDS CHAIN CODE: CU
AMADEUS CU ROMSOL
GALILEO CU 26784
SABRE CU 9364
WORLDSPAN CU SOLE

WWW.CHARMINGHOTELS.COM
+39 06 977 4591

ALBERGO DEL SOLE
AL PANTHEON ★★★★

HOTEL SOLE AL PANTHEON

This landmark hotel, dating from the 15th century, is one of the oldest in Rome. It has a truly stunning position in front of the Pantheon, the temple rebuilt by Hadrian in the 2nd century AD. Originally called The Ram Inn, the hotel's symbol of rams' horns can be seen on some of the silverware in the lobby, and on lampshades and other pieces of furniture. It later became known as the Sun Inn and was frequented by many distinguished visitors including the poet Ariosto, Jean-Paul Sartre and Simone de Beauvoir.

The historic building has been expertly restored with meticulous attention to detail. The high-ceilinged entrance hall with its terracotta tiled floor and whitewashed walls retains much of the hotel's original character. The comfortable public rooms maintain the same simple elegance of white walls decorated with beautiful oil paintings and white-upholstered furniture and antiques.

Like the public rooms, the individually decorated bedrooms retain their 15th-century character and are sumptuously furnished with canopied beds and antiques, though the amenities reflect 21st-century needs, with jacuzzis, satellite TV and air conditioning.

Breakfast is served in a tranquil garden patio off the inner courtyard; in summer it is served on the restaurant terrace. The bar serves snacks and sandwiches as well as coffee and drinks.

Residenza Torre Colonna

Via delle Tre Cannelle, 18
00187 Rome
www.charminghotels.com/torrecolonna

General Manager
Gianni Montanari
and Sarah Hawker

Open all year

Rooms & Facilities
5 rooms
Rooftop jacuzzi

Rates
Single from €140 to 170
Double from €200 to 230

Credit Cards
Visa, MasterCard, American Express, Carta Si, Diners, Maestro Card

Airports
Rome Fiumicino (FCO)
29 km/18 miles
Rome Ciampino (CIA)
20km/13 miles

Train Station
Rome Termini 2.3 km/1.4 miles

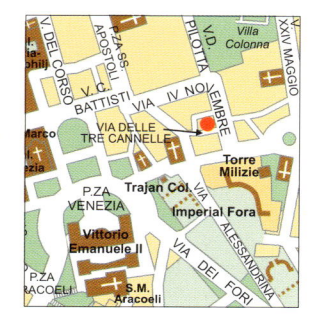

WWW.CHARMINGHOTELS.COM
+39 06 977 4591

Residenza Torre Colonna

The stalwart 13th-century Torre Colonna, once a defensive tower on the extensive city property of the Colonna family, has been masterfully transformed into an amazingly stylish and comfortable five-bedroom guest house, in a perfect central location near Piazza Venezia.

Though externally austere-looking, inside the conversion has been thoughtful and imaginative, with painstaking attention to detail. The rooms, one per floor, are large with stunningly minimalist décor, including wrought iron canopied beds, natural stone walls, exposed beams and staircases, perfectly complementing the medieval character of the original building. The atmosphere is luxurious, welcoming and comfortable.

Breakfast is served at the top of the building in a dramatically painted red room, with leather sofas, from which a glass spiral staircase rises to the roof terrace. Here there is a jaccuzi tub, a truly stunning place from which to appreciate the views of Trajan's Column, the Vittorio Emanuele monument and the Colosseum.

The Torre Colonna is also the showcase for contemporary Italian artist Natino Chirico, many of whose striking works hang throughout the tower.

Sarah Hawker
Owner

Hotel Villa Morgagni
Via G.B. Morgagni, 25
00161 Rome
www.charminghotels.com/villamorgagni

General Manager
Mrs Simona Gargari

Open all year

Rooms & Facilities
34 Rooms and suites
Bar
Spa services, sauna and Turkish bath
Jacuzzi in some rooms

Rates
Single from €95 to 150
Double from €120 to 260
Junior Suite from €150 to 280
VAT, breakfast & service charge included

Meeting Rooms: 1
Capacity: 50 max
Packages rates: on request

Credit Cards
Visa, MasterCard, American Express, Diners

Airports
Rome Fiumicino (FCO)
30 km/18 miles
Rome Ciampino (CIA)
20km/13 miles

Train Station
Rome Termini
2 km/1.2 miles

GDS CHAIN CODE: CU
AMADEUS CU ROMH69
GALILEO CU 54585
SABRE CU 34331
WORLDSPAN CU ROM69

WWW.CHARMINGHOTELS.COM
+39 06 977 4591

Hotel Villa Morgagni

The elegant, Liberty-style 19th-century Villa Morgagni is just beyond the centre of Rome in a very pleasant leafy residential area, near the 700-year-old Baths of Diocletian, the park of the Villa Torlonia and the university (La Sapienza). Set back from the busy main road by a long driveway, the hotel offers the peace and relaxation not always easy to find in bustling city-centre hotels. Excellent transport links, including the metro (the Policlinico stop is just a short walk away), bus lines and taxis, take visitors to the historic centre in minutes.

The 34 guest rooms, recently refurbished to create a balance of welcoming hospitality and elegance, have light-coloured walls and natural wood floors, and all are very tastefully decorated with warm, terracotta-coloured fabrics, tapestries and period furnishing combining elegance with comfort. Some rooms have private terraces, while others overlook the gardens of neighbouring properties. An extensive breakfast is served in the delightful rooftop garden. All the bedrooms are well equipped with satellite television and air conditioning; there is also a sauna and Turkish bath.

There are also full facilities, including a fully-equipped conference room, for business travellers.

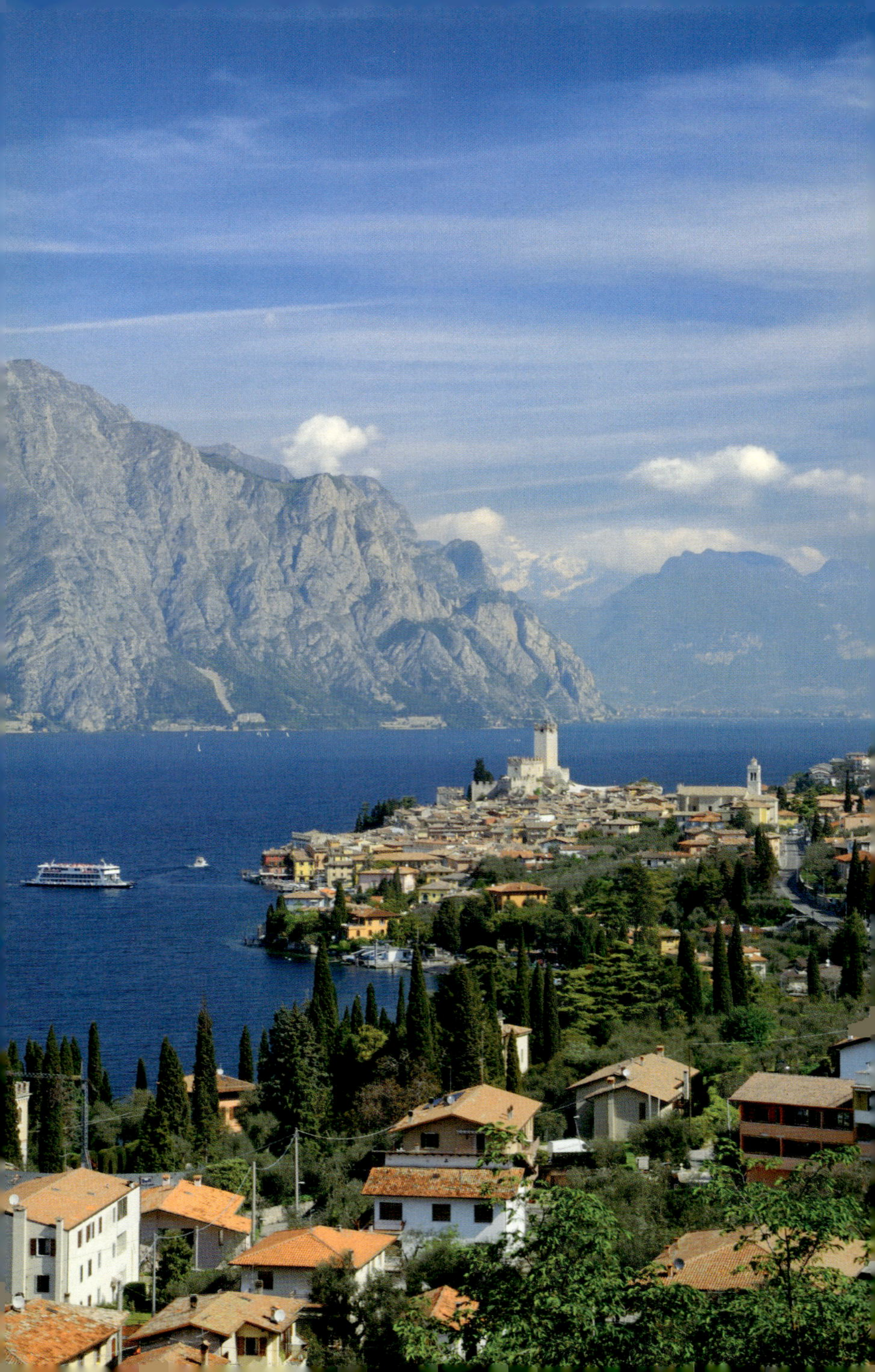

① Hotel Villa del Sogno p.64

Lombardy

THE LAKES

Lombardy is a prosperous region. The countryside is criss-crossed with waterways, which in the Middle Ages were fully navigable and many of the main towns acted as ports. The great lakes enjoy a microclimate which promotes splendid vegetation. The scenery around the lakes is some of the best in Italy.

LAKE GARDA The largest of the Italian lakes, Lake Garda has long been a place to rest and relax. The poet Catullus (d. 54 BC) had an extensive villa at Sirmione, the ruins of which can still be visited, while Goethe was famously infatuated with the lake. So huge is the lake (in bad weather, waves make it look like the sea) that it creates its own distinctive microclimate, which encourages a wide range of vegetation to flourish including orange and lemon trees, olives, cypresses and vines.

By the end of the 19th century the tiny village of Gardone Riviera had become famous as a winter resort, thanks largely to an Austrian, Luigi Wimmer, who having spent time here on an extended rest cure, decided to build a hotel. Advertising the benefits of both the lake and his hotel, he attracted wealthy Europeans, who came here for the particularly mild climate of the western shore. They in turn built villas of their own, and the place still has a pleasantly refined atmosphere.

Close by in Gardone is Gabriele d'Annunzio's residence and mausoleum, the Vittoriale degli Italiani, filled with the poet's eclectic possessions which included more than 10,000 works of art and more than 33,000 books. An amphitheatre is hidden the gardens, along with the prow of the ship *Puglia*, which was placed here as a monument.

In the nearby countryside there are many beautiful gardens to explore and walks with stunning views of the lake.

Lake Garda

HISTORY Lake Garda was known to the Romans as Lacus Benacus and there were settlements dotted around the shore, including those at Sirmione and Desenzano. Many of the lake-side towns have castles built by the Scaligeri family, the ruling family of Verona. The local economy of citrus fruit growing was displaced by tourism as the lake became a popular stop on the Grand Tour.

CULTURE Until the 18th and 19th centuries when tourism began to take a hold, this area of the lake was famous for the growing of citrus fruit, this being the most northerly point where it was possible to do so commercially. The economy was supplemented by fishing; the lake contains *Salmo carpio*, a fish unique to Lake Garda.

FOOD Fish from the lake features on most menus, and there is plenty of choice: trout, eel and bass, cooked as a sauce for pasta, but also fried or grilled with herbs. Lemons are used in the usually light seasoning, along with local olive oil. Local wines from Bardolino and the southern area of the lake are excellent.

EVENTS July: music festival at Salò.
July and August: Festival d'Estate, summer festival of opera, music and dance at the Teatro del Vittoriale.

TRANSPORTATION The nearest airports are those at Milan and Verona/Brescia. The Milan–Venice railway line runs along the southern edge of the lake with stops at Desenzano and Sirmione. A daily bus service run along the west and east side of the lake, calling at all major towns. Boat services operate on the lake, including two modernised paddle steamers in the summer.

POPULATION GARDONE RIVIERA: 2,500
AREA CODE: + 39 0365
TOURIST OFFICE: + 39 0365 20347
www.bresciaholiday.com

63

Hotel Villa del Sogno
Via Zanardelli, 107
25083 Gardone Riviera
www.charminghotels.com/
hotelvilladelsogno

General Manager
Mr Davide Calderan

Open
April to October

Rooms & Facilities
35 Rooms and suites
Garden bar at pool
Extensive shaded park
Panoramic terrace
with view of Lake Garda
Wellness centre

Rates
Double Single Use from
€203 to 259
Double from €290 to 420
Junior Suite from €390 to 520
VAT, breakfast & service
charge included

Dining
Maximilian 1904 Restaurant
American Bar

Meeting Rooms: 1
Capacity: 30 max
Package rates: on request

Credit Cards
Visa, MasterCard,
American Express, Diners

Airports
Verona Airport (VRN)
60 km/37 miles
Milan Malpensa (MXP)
150 km/93 miles

Train Station
Desenzano
25 km/15 miles

GDS CHAIN CODE: CU
AMADEUS CU VRNOGN
GALILEO CU 50736
SABRE CU 5428
WORLDSPAN CU SOGN

WWW.CHARMINGHOTELS.COM
+39 06 977 4591

Hotel Villa del Sogno

Surrounded by its own extensive parkland, with hidden temples and secluded walks, and with magnificent views of Lake Garda, Hotel Villa del Sogno has been superbly restored to its original *fin-de-siècle* style. Originally the private home of a wealthy German silk manufacturer, it still retains the relaxed, intimate atmosphere of a country retreat.

The hotel offers a choice of accommodation, from comfortable standard rooms to suites with gym, jacuzzi, massage bed and private terrace. All rooms are decorated to the very highest standards of comfort and elegance, and in a variety of styles: Venetian, Liberty, Biedermeier. There is also a swimming pool, a wellness centre offering a wide range of natural beauty and relaxation treatments, and tennis courts.

Hotel Villa del Sogno has a selection of places to eat and drink; the informal Garden Bar serves the finest wines and simple, light Italian dishes throughout the day, while the Maximilian Restaurant, with magnificent view of the lake from the terrace, offers more formal dining in the evening, offering typical Italian dishes reinvented with contemporary flair and imagination. The American Bar is open till late serving a wide range of liqueurs and digestifs.

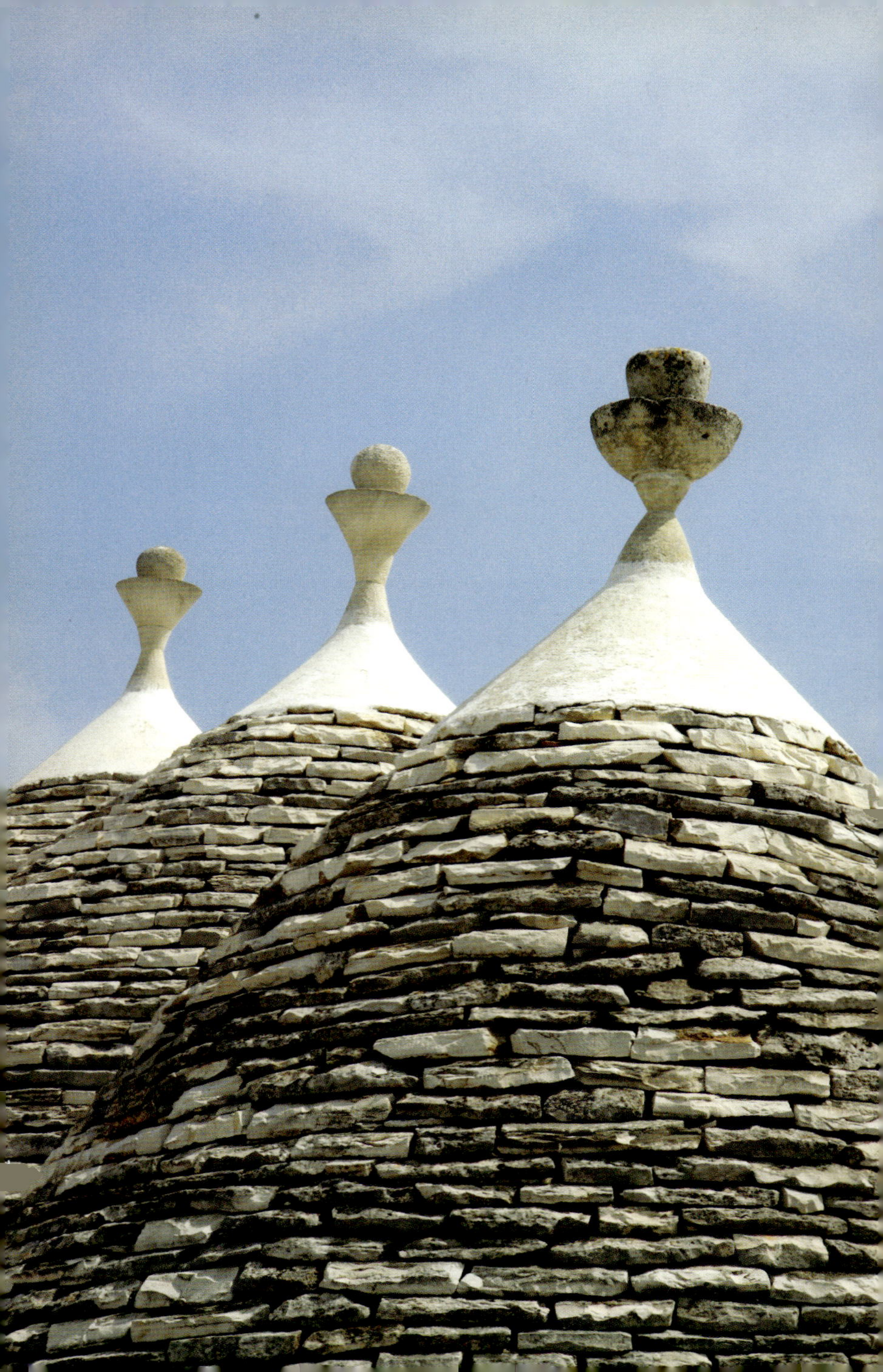

1. ALBOREA ECO LODGE p.72
2. GRAND HOTEL KALIDRIA p.74

Puglia

There are many influences that have gone to make up Puglia. Roman, Byzantine, Arab and Norman rule all made a distinct and lasting impression on the region. It is now the richest and most dynamic region of Southern Italy. Bari, Alberobello, Lecce and Otranto are all worth a visit.

CASTELLANETA MARINA Situated on the shores of Gulf of Taranto, Castellaneta Marina is a typical southern Mediterranean seaside resort of endless white sand, close to the Stornara Nature Reserve. This reserve was created in 1997 to preserve the native Aleppo pines of the coastal forest which can tolerate the high temperatures and dry climate of the region. The shrubs which grow in the forest give off a particularly evocative fragrance and are home to numberless cicadas; in winter it is home to tens of thousands of migrating starlings, which give the reserve its name.

Castellaneta Marina is 25km from historic Taranto, which started life as the Greek town of Taras, a colony of Sparta which was established in the 8th century BC and became the greatest city in Magna Graecia, the name given to Greek-colonized southern Italy before it was absorbed into the Roman Empire. Today it is an important commercial port and industrial centre. But it is worth visiting for the magnificent hoard of Taranto gold, a collection of beautiful objects of gold and precious metals and stones.

Along the coast to the west of Castellaneta Marina is the site of ancient Metapontum, founded in the 7th century BC. After he had been expelled from Croton, Pythagoras re-established his school of philosophy here around 510 BC.

Castellaneta Marina

HISTORY After the defeat of Taras (modern Taranto), centre of the refined Greek culture in the region, Puglia prospered under Roman control. Years of Byzantine rule after the fall of the Western Roman Empire, reinforced the region's decidedly Greek character. In later centuries it fell under the influence of Naples and Sicily.

CULTURE With their conical roofs and white-washed, dry-stone walls, *trulli* are unusual dwellings characteristic of the region. The images often seen on the grey roof-tiles are thought to have religious or folkloric significance.

FOOD As well as the traditional Italian staples of excellent olive oil, delicious fresh vegetables and fruit, Puglia also grows wheat, which is made into some of Italy's finest bread. At the eastern tip of the Italian peninsula, the region's cuisine has benefited from the influences of ingredients and flavours from East and North Africa.

EVENTS Taranto, Maundy Thursday–Easter Sunday: Holy Week celebrations
10th May: festival of San Cataldo when a statue of the saint is carried in a warship, followed by local boats. Finishes with fireworks and the eating of *carteddate*, pastry made with wine. First Sunday in September: festival of Stella Maris, when a statue of the Virgin is taken out to sea.

TRANSPORTATION
The main airports which serve this area are Bari, Brindisi and Foggia.
The main railway runs to Taranto from Bari.
The E90 road runs along the coast behind the resort.

POPULATION: 17,000
AREA CODE: + 39 099
TOURIST OFFICE: +39 099 453 2397
WWW.APT.TA.IT

Alborea Eco Lodge
Località Principessa
S.S. 106, km 466.6
74010 Castellaneta Marina
www.charminghotels.com/alborea

General Manager
Mr Vincenzo Gentile

Open From
29th May 2010

Rooms & Facilities
124 Eco Lodge Suites
Thalasso spa
Fitness centre
Private beach

Rates
Single from €150 to 292
Double from €200 to 390
Lodge Superior plus €100 per lodge per day
VAT, HB & service charge included

Dining
2 bars and 5 restaurants

Meeting Rooms: 30
Capacity: 600 max
Package rates: on request

Credit Cards
Visa, MasterCard, American Express, CartaSi, Diners, Maestro Card

Airports
Bari Airport (BRI)
100 km/62 miles
Brindisi Airport (BDS)
90 km/56 miles

Train Stations
Taranto
25 km/15.5 miles
Castellaneta
20 km/12 miles
Bari
100 km/62 miles

WWW.CHARMINGHOTELS.COM
+39 06 977 4591

ALBOREA
ECO LODGE SUITES

Alborea Eco Lodge

Part of the extensive Nova Yardinia Resort and set in 16 hectares of natural parkland, this is the ultimate place for peace and relaxation, on the edge of the Stornara Nature Reserve and overlooking the Bay of Taranto. The 124 independent eco-lodges are set in the natural clearings of pine trees and wild herbs, successfully combining nature, design and comfort. All are spacious with light, modern wooden furniture, verandas, panoramic windows and hydro-massage baths.

The complex offers a choice of places to eat. The Silvo grill restaurant serves an extensive breakfast while the wide-ranging dinner menu is inspired by flavours and ingredients from Greece, Spain and France as well as Italy. Light meals and snacks, fruit and delicious traditional Italian ice-cream is served from the Taresco poolside bar.

A delightful short walk through the aromatic pine trees leads to a private beach with fine white sand, sun loungers, parasols and bar service.

The heated indoor and outdoor sea-water swimming pools and all the thalasso spa facilities of the neighbouring Hotel Kalidria are available to everyone staying at Alborea.

Grand Hotel Kalidria

Località Principessa
S.S. 106, km 466.6
74010 Castellaneta Marina
www.charminghotels.com/grandhotelkalidria

General Manager
Mr Vincenzo Gentile

Open
1st November to
15th December (2010)

Rooms & Facilities
110 Rooms and Suites
Thalasso spa
Fitness centre
Private beach

Rates
Single from €113 to 173
Double from €150 to 270
Suite from €210 to 330
VAT, breakfast & service charge included

Dining
2 bars and 5 restaurants

Meeting Rooms: 30
Capacity: 600 max
Package rates: on request

Credit Cards
Visa, MasterCard, American Express, CartaSi, Diners, Maestro Card

Airports
Bari Airport (BRI)
100 km/62 miles
Brindisi Airport (BDS)
90 km/56 miles

Train Stations
Taranto
25 km/15.5 miles
Castellaneta
20 km/12 miles
Bari
100 km/62 miles

GDS CHAIN CODE: CU
AMADEUS CU BRIKAL
GALILEO CU 6216
SABRE CU 62066
WORLDSPAN CU BRIKA

WWW.CHARMINGHOTELS.COM
+39 06 977 4591

KALIDRIA
GRAND HOTEL & THALASSO SPA

Grand Hotel Kalidria & Thalasso Spa

The dazzling, ultra-modern Grand Hotel Kalidria overlooks the Gulf of Taranto. Its elegant, spacious rooms, built around the large swimming pool with stunning views over the fragrant Aleppo pine trees of the Stornara Nature Reserve, are cool and stylish, promoting rest and relaxation. There are private balconies equipped with sun loungers.

The thalasso spa centre, Nova Yardinia, has heated indoor and outdoor sea-water pools and a state-of-the-art, fully-equipped fitness and beauty centre, with specialists to advise on personalized health training programs, including *remise en forme*, a mother's wellness program and anti-stress remedies. It offers an amazing choice of thalasso-therapies as well as traditional treatments such as saunas, Turkish baths and massage.

The restaurants promote healthy eating but never compromise on taste, creating imaginative menus combining the rich flavours and colours of locally-inspired dishes using the only the very finest and freshest ingredients.

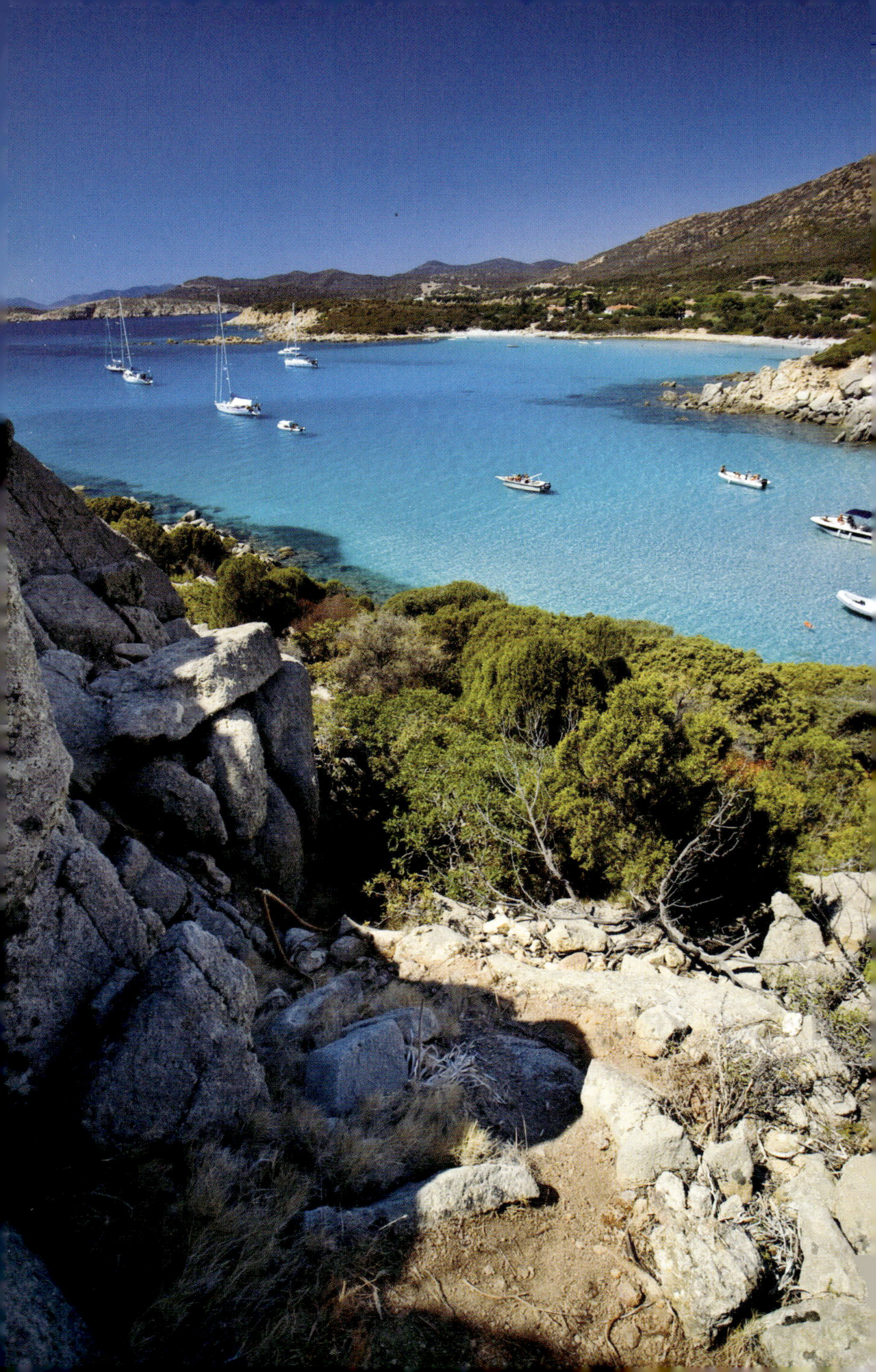

1. HOTEL CAPO D'ORSO THALASSO & SPA p.82
2. VALLE DELL'ERICA RESORT THALASSO & SPA p.88

Sardinia

Sardinia is a captivating island of rugged natural beauty, an enticing blend of contrast and variety. The dramatic coastline conceals hidden coves and remote sandy bays, while the lush interior, with historic remains, vineyards and isolated farmhouses, is an unspoilt walker's paradise.

CALA CAPRA Sardinia is the second largest island in the Mediterranean with a high, rocky coastline and many hidden inlets and breathtaking views from the head-lands. The secluded resort of Cala Capra, which means 'goat's head', sits in one of these inlets, located in on tiny peninsula, a perfect crescent of fine white sand, fringed with pine trees and aromatic Mediterranean *macchia*. Across the bay there are fine views of the archipelago of La Maddalena, and away to the east, the beautiful Costa Smeralda.

With its gently shelving beach, crystal clear waters and hidden coves, this is a perfect place for swimmers, snorkellers and scuba divers, and there are boat trips to explore the islets of La Maddalena and around the coast. From the amazing granite Capo d'Orso rock, which overlooks the beach, sculpted by the elements over thousands of years into the unmistakable shape of a bear, there are stunning views across to Corsica. This is ideal walking country, through cool pines and juniper and olive groves.

The nearest town is Palau, about 4km away, with its bustling harbour busy with ferries from Corsica and La Maddalena, and a colourful weekly market. Inland from Palau, near Arzachena, are amazing relics from the Nuraghic age, a civilisation dating between the Bronze Age and Iron Ages, including towers, dolmens, graves and stone circles.

Cala Capra

HISTORY The earliest settlers on Sardinia probably came from Etruria. Later, villages were established around the *nuraghi*, the tower fortresses of the Nuraghic people. Their purpose is not known, but around 8,000 out of an original 15,000 still exist on the island, along with dolmens, tombs, menhirs, cisterns and other evidence of life between 1800 and 500 BC.

CULTURE With its rocky coastline and the threat of pirate raids, the northeast of the island has been a place for farmers and shepherds rather than fishermen. Sheep and goats have grazed on the plateau above Cala Capra for generations, producing flavoursome cheeses, including *Pecorino Sardo*. The shepherds' thatched-roofed huts can be seen in many fields in the area.

FOOD Unlike many islands in the Mediterranean, Sardinia does not rely on the sea for its cuisine. Wheat grown on the fertile uplands is used to make the delicious bread which goes into *suppa cuata*, or 'hidden soup'. Succulent lamb and suckling pig, fed on the aromatic vegetation of the island, are grilled with rosemary and other wild herbs; sheep and goats' milk produces distinctive tangy cheeses.

EVENTS May, second last Sunday: Cavalcata Sarda is Sardinia's most important music festival, when traditional costumes and jewellery are worn. Holy Week is celebrated in many parts of the island, with re-enactments of the Passion of Christ. 15th August: feast of the Assumption. September, first week: Barefoot Run and Festival of San Salvatore, nine days of celebrations.

TRANSPORTATION
The island's main airport is at Cagliari in the south of the island. The nearest airport to Cala Capra, with taxis and car hire, is at Olbia, 40km from Palau; there are regular shuttle buses to the town. There is one bus a day from the airport to Santa Teresa di Gallura which stops at Palau. Trains from Palau run to Arzachena. Ferry services go to Genoa and La Maddalena.

POPULATION:
4,000
AREA CODE:
+ 39 0789
TOURIST OFFICE:
+39 789557732
WWW.PALAU.IT
WWW.PALAUSARDINIA.COM
WWW.SARDEGNATURISMO.IT

Hotel Capo d'Orso Thalasso & Spa
Cala Capra
07020 Palau
www.charminghotels.com/hotelcapodorso

General Manager
Mr Luca Cagliero

Open
23rd May to 4th October

Rooms & Facilities
84 Rooms and suites
Open air gym
Golf (Pitch & Putt), 9 holes

Rates
Double Single Use from €210 to 540
Double from €150 to 390 p.p.
Junior Suite from €180 to 500 p.p.
VAT, HB & service charge included

Dining
Il Paguro Restaurant
Gli Olivastri Restaurant
L'Approdo Snack Bar
Piano Bar
Thalasso & Spa Centre

Meeting Rooms: 1
Capacity: 150 max
Package rates: on request

Credit Cards
Visa, MasterCard, CartaSi
American Express, Eurocard

Airport
Olbia Airport (OLB)
42 km/26 miles

Train Station
Olbia
42 km/26 miles

GDS CHAIN CODE: CU
AMADEUS CU OLBRSO
GALILEO CU 57297
SABRE CU 34701
WORLDSPAN CU ORSO

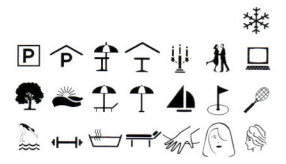

WWW.CHARMINGHOTELS.COM
+39 06 977 4591

Hotel Capo d'Orso
Thalasso & Spa

The secluded Hotel Capo d'Orso, set in private parkland of wild olive groves and juniper woods, overlooks the sparkling Cala Capra Bay on the glorious Costa Smeralda. This is a truly unspoilt corner of Sardinia, just a few metres from the sea, and the hotel has been carefully designed to take advantage of and blend in with, the natural features of this glorious landscape.

The hotel has 84 rooms and suites, designed and furnished by local architects. The theme of the rooms throughout is stylish simplicity—pale-coloured walls, tiled floors, canopied beds—while never compromising comfort.

There is a choice of three restaurants: Il Paguro ('The Hermit Crab') is a cosy place overlooking the sea specialising in seafood. For a more formal occasion Gli Olivastri ('The Olives') is romantically set among the ancient olive trees. L'Approdo ('The Landing Stage') serves delicious pizza cooked in traditional wood-fired ovens. Breakfast, accompanied by a harpist, is served on the terrace overlooking the sea.

The hotel offers a wide range of services including a gym, a relaxing thalasso spa with a variety of therapies, and a private beach and marina.

SANTA TERESA GALLURA sits at the very tip of northern Sardinia, overlooking the Straits of Bonifacio. From the beach the coast of Corsica can clearly be seen on the horizon and ferries shuttle between the busy little harbour and the French island. A choice of beautiful white sandy beaches, hidden coves and a relaxed atmosphere make this a popular destination. The clear turquoise blue waters are a paradise for swimmers and snorkellers. Behind this pretty little town there are walks among the weather-beaten hills, sculpted into extraordinary shapes by the wind and rain of millennia. The nearby Capo Testa promontory has been smoothed by the elements to reveal the unexpectedly vibrant underlying colours of the granite. *Valle della Luna* (Moon Valley) is a massive fault in the rock, further widened by years of erosion.

Further inland there is ample evidence of the prehistoric peoples who settled in this region. The solid stone towers and settlements dating from the Nuraghic period of the island's civilisation can still be seen, along with evidence of their village settlements, temples and dolmens.

The largest town in the region is Olbia, with shops, restaurants and a busy port. The cathedral, the basilica of San Simplicio, was built on a hill in the 11th century and is made of the local granite, which was also used for the columns of the Pantheon in Rome.

Santa Teresa Gallura

HISTORY Settled in the earliest times by the Nuraghic people, it was conquered by the Romans and in the Middle Ages was of importance to the Pisans, whose rivals the Genoese ruled Corsica. Destroyed by the Genoese, the area became a refuge for smugglers until 1808 when, to drive out the pirates, King Vittorio Emanuele instigated the establishment of Santa Teresa Gallura, offering settlers free plots of land.

CULTURE One of the island's more unusual traditions is the Barefoot Run in September. On the first Saturday of the month around 1,000 runners, all barefoot and wearing white robes, carry an image of San Salvatore 7km from the church of Santa Maria Assunta in Cabras to the saint's church in the village of San Salvatore. On the next day, the image is returned to Cabras followed by an evening's celebration.

FOOD Food in the northeastern part of the island is deliciously simple. A typical speciality is *suppa cuata* or *suppa gallurese*, not really a soup at all but layers of bread and soft cheese soaked in meat stock and baked in the oven. Being an agricultural region, pork, lamb and kid are the most usual meats, grilled with herbs or used in casseroles, delicious when accompanied by one of Sardinia's many wines.

EVENTS Easter: there are many moving celebrations over the Easter period. March: end of the month citrus festival at Muravera, with colourful folk costumes and local crafts as well as displays of the finest citrus fruits. 28th April: Sa Die de Sa Sardigna, celebrations to commemorate Sardinia Day. August, first Sunday: Vermentino Festival, two days celebrating and sampling the famous wine and local cuisine.

TRANSPORTATION
The island's main airport is at Cagliari in the south. The nearest airport, with taxis and car hire, is at Olbia; there are regular shuttle buses to town. There is one bus a day from the airport to Santa Teresa Gallura. Trains from Palau run to Arzachena and then further inland. Ferry services run from Santa Teresa Gallura to Corsica (Bonifacio) and La Maddalena.

POPULATION: 5,000
AREA CODE: + 39 0789
TOURIST OFFICE: + 39 789557732
www.sardegnaturismo.it

Valle dell'Erica Resort Thalasso & Spa

Valle dell'Erica
07028 Santa Teresa Gallura
Olbia–Tempio
www.charminghotels.com/resortvalledellerica

General Manager
Giuseppe Antonio Panunzio

Open
22nd May to 18th September

Rooms & Facilities
140 Rooms and suites
Thalasso & spa centre
Golf: 18 holes Putt & Putt;
3 holes Pitch & Putt

Rates
Double Single Use from €190 to 490
Double from €140 to 300 p.p.
Junior Suite to €180 to 400 p.p.
VAT, HB & service charge included

Dining
2 Restaurants
2 Bars

Credit Cards
Visa, MasterCard, American Express, CartaSi, Euro Card

Airport
Olbia Airport (OLB)
55 km/34 miles

Train Station
Olbia
55 km/34 miles

GDS CHAIN CODE: CU
AMADEUS CU OLBRIC
GALILEO CU 39508
SABRE CU 51138
WORLDSPAN CU OLBER

WWW.CHARMINGHOTELS.COM
+39 06 977 4591

Valle dell'Erica
Resort Thalasso & Spa

Created in the late 1950s this was the first tourist village on the island and very quickly became a stylish and sophisticated holiday resort. It was thoroughly refurbished in 2005, adapting and improving the standards of the original buildings, equipping them with all modern amenities, while respecting the natural ecology of the landscape.

Close to white sandy bays and numerous secluded coves overlooking the Straits of Bonifacio, the resort has 140 rooms including junior suites, all on the ground floor with independent entrances. All rooms are furnished in Mediterranean style with private verandas and equipped with sun loungers (or chairs).

Breakfast is served on the terrace overlooking the sea, while the main restaurant, with its amazing views across the whole archipelago of La Maddalena, offers an extensive and varied buffet. In the summer, the fresh catch of the day is served directly on the beach (on request and at an extra charge).

The thalasso spa area, Le Thermae, is situated in the natural granite rocks, with four sea-water swimming pools at different temperatures; there are cabins for thalasso-therapy treatments and saunas, Turkish baths and massage.

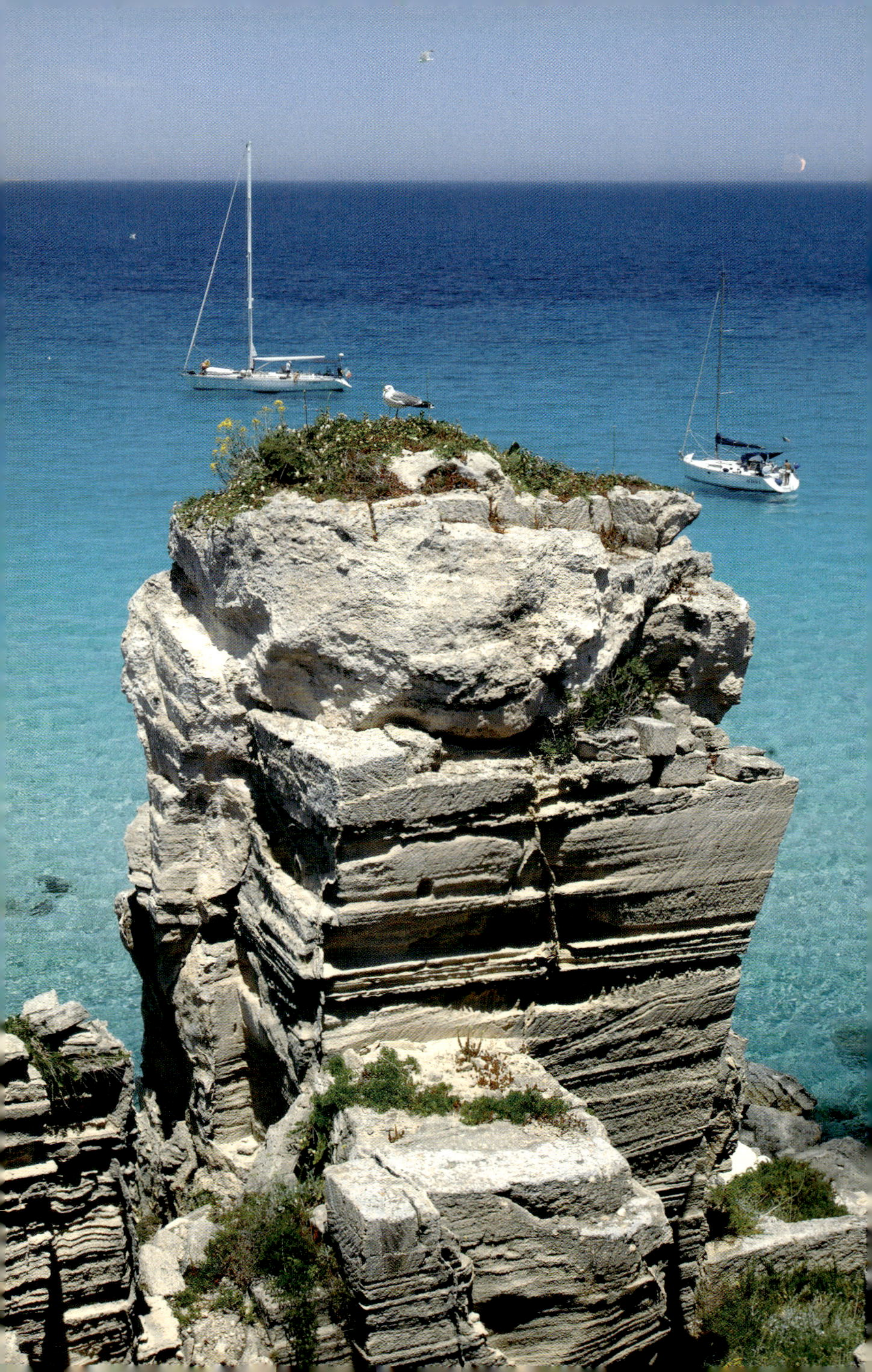

1 CAVE BIANCHE HOTEL p.96

Sicily

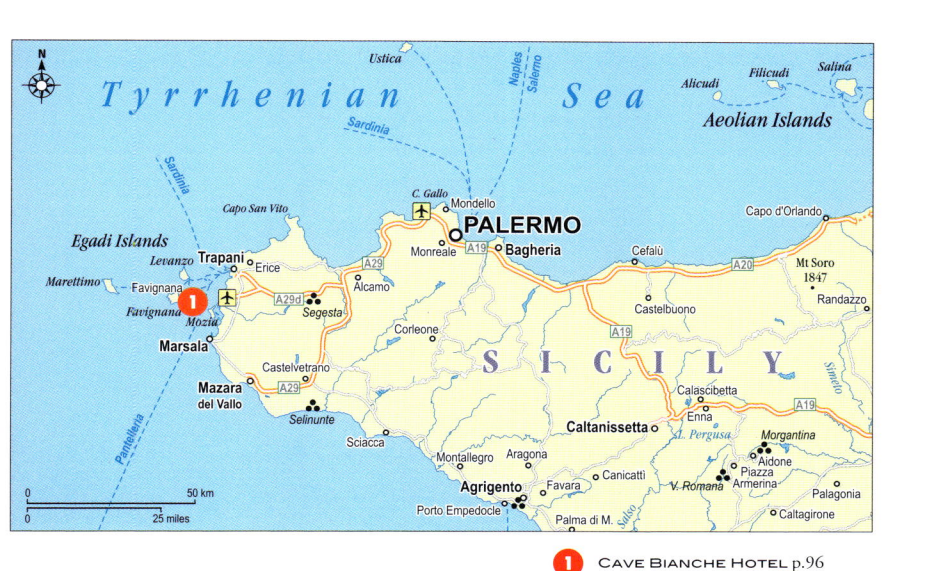

Goethe once said 'To understand Italy you must see Sicily.' He was referring to Sicily's complex history, a concentration of everything that happened in Italy. Now Sicily and the Egadi Islands are major tourist destinations, popular for their wealth of ancient ruins, their cuisine and for their beautiful beaches.

FAVIGNANA is the largest of the three Egadi Islands, which lie off the west coast of Sicily. Such is their importance to the migratory birdlife which passes through in the spring and autumn each year, that these islands have been declared a maritime nature reserve, the largest in Italy.

Just 17km southwest of Trapani on Sicily, butterfly-shaped Favignana is mostly flat and given over to pasture and scrub. The pretty little medieval town of Favignana is where most people on the island live and where passenger and fishing boats dock. The striking Art Nouveau Palazzo Florio, set back from the harbour, belonged to Ignazio Florio, who owned the massive Tonnara Florio at the other end of the harbour, where tuna was processed until just a few years ago. A statue of Ignazio stands proudly in front of the town hall, an attractive 19th-century *palazzo*. On a hill overlooking the town and harbour sits Fort Santa Caterina, built by the Saracens as a watchtower, refortified by the Normans, and during Bourbon rule used as a prison. It is still used for military purposes today.

To the east of the island there is still evidence of the tufa quarries which were an important part of the local economy but today only one remains in business. The coast has many rocky bays, including Cala Rossa on the northeast. There are sandier and more popular beaches on the south.

Favignana

HISTORY The Egadi Islands are known to have been inhabited since prehistoric times (the island of Levanzo has some amazing cave paintings) and it was in these waters that Lutatius Catulus routed the fleet of Hanno, bringing about one of the most decisive victories over Carthage which ended the first Punic War in 241 BC.

CULTURE As tufa quarrying comes to an end, some of the disused quarries have been reclaimed and turned into 'secret' gardens. Sheltered from the high winds that often batter the island, more than 200 different species of plants and trees flourish in these peaceful sunken oases.

FOOD Although no longer fished commercially here, tuna is still an important ingredient, prepared in a seemingly endless variety of ways. The cuisine here borrows from that of Trapani, adding its own distinctive touch, including fish couscous using delicate sea bass, served with a lobster broth.

EVENTS 14th September: feast of the Santissimo Crocifisso, the most important festival on the island.

TRANSPORTATION
Ferries and hydrofoil services operate regularly from Trapani. Trapani is an hour away from Palermo airport.

POPULATION: 4,000
AREA CODE: +39 0923
TOURIST OFFICE: + 39 0923 921647
WWW.TRAPANI-SICILIA.IT
WWW.EGADIWEB.IT

Cave Bianche Hotel
Strada Comunale Fanfalo
91023 Favignana
www.charminghotels.com/cavebianchehotel

General Manager
Mr Livio Gandolfo

Open
1st April to 30th October

Rooms & Facilities
32 Rooms
Bar
Outdoor swimming pool,
Outdoor heated swimming pool

Rates
Single from €69 to 149
Double from €126 to 366
VAT, breakfast & service charge included

Dining
Cave Bianche Restaurant

Credit Cards
Visa, MasterCard,
American Express, Diners

Airports
Trapani V. Florio (TPS)
18 km/11 miles
Palermo Falcone Borsellino (PMO)
80 km/50 miles

GDS CHAIN CODE: CU
AMADEUS CU TPSGAD
GALILEO CU 72406
SABRE CU 44578
WORLDSPAN CU EGAD

WWW.CHARMINGHOTELS.COM
+39 06 977 4591

Cave Bianche Hotel

On the tiny island of Favignana, the ingeniously designed Cave Bianche Hotel has been built within the white walls of an ancient calcarenite quarry, creating a perfect cool, peaceful retreat.

This sleek, ultra-modern boutique hotel was built using natural, eco-friendly materials with the aim of maintaining an environmental balance wherever possible: the water is mixed with air to reduce consumption and is heated by solar power.

The rooms are comfortably stylish and simply furnished, though never compromising comfort, with natural stone walls and floors; the furniture is contemporary and minimal, decorated using non-toxic paints.

The grounds are beautifully landscaped and planted with fragrant lemon and orange trees, oleanders and figs. There is a swimming pool, hydro-massage pools and a solarium.

Light lunches of imaginative salads and fresh fruit are served on the terrace, while in the evening typical Mediterranean dishes, with an emphasis on locally-caught fish, are accompanied by a wide choice of the best Sicilian wines.

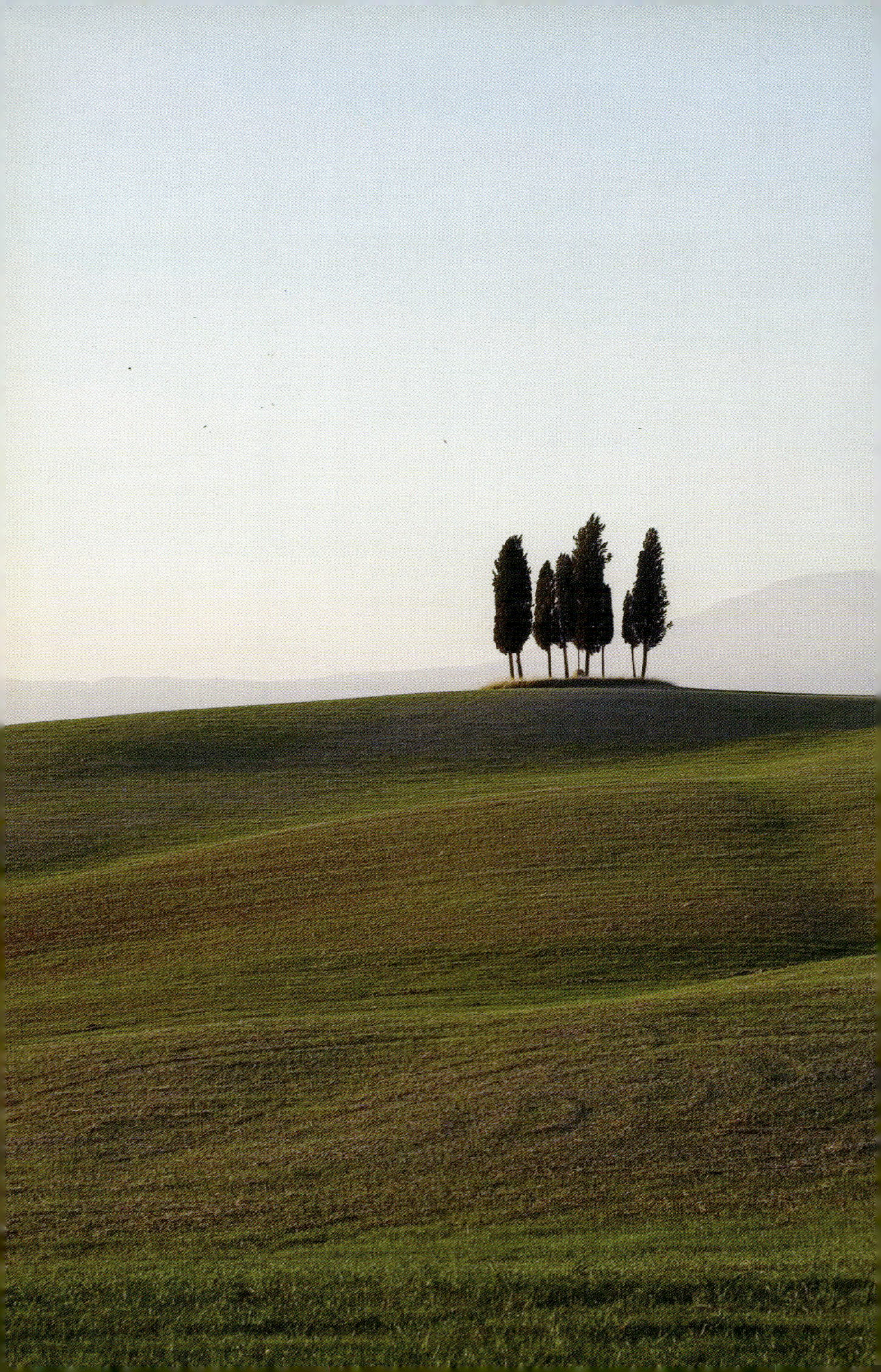

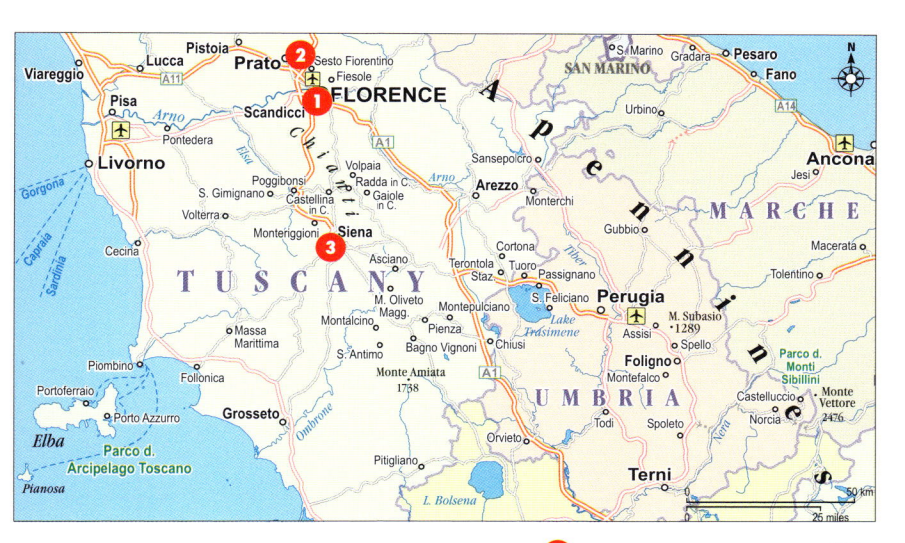

1. HOTEL HELVETIA & BRISTOL p.106
2. VILLA STANLEY p.108
3. GRAND HOTEL CONTINENTAL p.116

Tuscany

For many people Tuscany is quintessentially Italy. Its landscape, climate and architecture inform our ideas of the entire country. It is where our understanding of European art begins. It is also the region of Florence, Siena and Pisa, the most popular destinations in Italy.

Florence & Sesto Fiorentino

As the birthplace of the Renaissance, home of Michelangelo, the Medici and Machiavelli, and showcase of some of the most important works of art and architecture in the world, Florence can be an overwhelming city. But it is also one of great charm and beauty. Set on the banks of the River Arno, the backdrop of the surrounding hills of olive groves and vineyards is a perfect contrast to the warm terracotta-coloured tiles of Brunelleschi's dome of Santa Maria del Fiore, Florence's cathedral. The duomo, with the contrasting marbles of its exterior, its slender detached campanile designed by Giotto, and the Baptistery are near-perfect examples of intellectual and artistic accomplishment.

The Uffizi is undisputedly one of the world's greatest art galleries, displaying 2,000 paintings from the medieval to the modern age, as well as sculptures, tapestries and miniatures. Within the walls of the solid, fortress-like *palazzi*, built as a testament to the power and wealth of the families who owned them, are further outstanding art collections. The city's churches are also treasure houses, including Masaccio's breathtaking frescoes in Santa Maria del Carmine, Michelangelo's tombs for the Medici in San Lorenzo and Giotto's works in Santa Croce. But there is more to Florence than her art. There are beautiful squares in which to while away a few hours, while appreciating some of the world's finest Renaissance architecture and peaceful, shady gardens and parks. Beyond the city there are pretty villages to discover, with captivating views back to the city.

Florence

HISTORY Though founded by Julius Caesar, Florence only rose to importance in the Middle Ages when, already a significant centre for the woollen cloth industry, it became an important centre for banking and finance. The Florentine government supported the Guelph party, mainly made up of the merchant class, and expanded the party's influence into Tuscany, conquering neighbouring Pisa, which gave Florence an important trading outlet to the sea.

By the 15th century the city was ruled by the Medici, the influential dynasty which led Florence to its intellectual, artistic and commercial supremacy. Although there were often strong republican moves against the family, the three wiliest members, Cosimo il Vecchio, Pietro and Lorenzo the Magnificent succeeded in balancing democracy with autocracy.

The Medici line died out in the 18th century and the city passed to the house of Lorraine, with Peter Leopold spearheading important civil and cultural reforms.

Florence became the capital of Italy in 1865, conceding the title to Rome six years later.

CULTURE In the 13th and 14th centuries, Florence's economy rested on its wool trade and the city became a vast market-place of fabrics of all sorts. Today, the city is still famous for its luxury goods. The Mercato Nuovo has been trading since the 11th century and Cosimo I paid for the loggia in 1547 when it sold mainly silks and gold. Today it is an excellent place for beautiful leather goods and scarves. The city has a number of good markets. The one around the church of San Lorenzo is also good for leather goods and shoes, scarves and clothes as well as souvenirs; that at Sant'Ambrogio is less well-known to tourists but is good for bargains.

There are exquisite designer shops along Via Tornabuoni and Via della Vigna Nuova. Gold and silversmiths have been selling their wares from the pretty shops on the Ponte Vecchio since 1593, while at the more modest end of the scale, beautiful hand-made marbled paper and other traditional crafts can be found in the Oltrarno.

Food Florence, the capital of Tuscany, sits at the heart of one of Italy's most abundant agricultural regions. The huge success of Tuscan cuisine, which still draws its inspiration from rural tradition, lies in the quality of the ingredients—soft olive oils, pecorino cheese, fresh vegetables—and the simplicity of their preparation. Chianina cattle graze on Tuscan pastureland and produce some of Italy's finest, most tender beef; *bistecca alla fiorentina* is traditional T-bone steak, cooked over charcoal, best served medium-rare. Beef is also used in *stracotto*, a rich, slow-cooked beef stew. *Fritto misto* is a delicious combination of fried rabbit, chicken and vegetables. Bread is an important part of Tuscan cuisine and is used in a variety of ways; in *pappa al pomodoro,* a soup made with bread cooked with tomatoes, garlic and basil. Bread is also the basis for *antipasti* such as *bruschette*, *crostini toscani, fettunta* and *panzanella*. Tuscan wines are justifiably world-renowned: Brunello di Montalcino and Vino Nobile di Montepulciano are among the finest reds, with a price to match, but the easy-drinking reds of Chianti region are extremely palatable.

Transportation

Florence airport is at Peretola, a few kilometres to the west of the city but most airlines operate from Pisa airport, from where there is a direct rail link to Florence's Santa Maria Novella train station.

There are good train links to the major Italian cities from Santa Maria Novella train station.

Public transport in the city is run by ATAF and LI-NEA; useful tourist routes include no. 7 from the station to Fiesole by way of San Marco and San Domenico, no. 11 with stops at the station, the Duomo and San Marco and no. 12/13 which stops at the station, Piazzale Michelangelo and San Miniato al Monte. Local buses to outlying towns and villages in Tuscany leave from outside the train station.

Population: 370,000
Area code: + 39 055
Tourist office: + 39 055 290832
www.firenzeturismo.it

Hotel
Helvetia & Bristol
Via dei Pescioni, 2
50123 Florence
www.charminghotels.com/hotelbristol

General Manager
Mr Stefano Venturi

Open all year

Rooms & Facilities
67 Rooms and suites
Jacuzzi baths in Junior Suites and Suites, WI-FI in all areas and rooms
Valet service

Rates
Superior Single from €180 to 240
Double from €195 to 435
Suite from €475 to 1725
VAT, buffet breakfast & service charge not included

Dining
Hostaria Bibendum Cocktail Bar & Restaurant

Meeting Rooms: 4
Capacity: 100 max
Package rates: on request

Credit Cards
Visa, MasterCard, American Express, Diners, JCB

Airport
Florence Airport (FLR)
9 km/5.6 miles

Train Station
Florence Santa Maria Novella
1 km/0.62 miles

WWW.CHARMINGHOTELS.COM
+39 06 977 4591

HOTEL HELVETIA & BRISTOL

Small and extremely elegant, the Helvetia & Bristol is an historic hotel in an outstanding position in the very centre of Florence, opposite the impressive Renaissance Palazzo Strozzi and near the city's best shopping street, Via Tornabuoni. Over 100 years old, it was home to many visitors on the Grand Tour and today it is still the epitome of luxury and impeccable service.

Alessandro Marchese
Head Concierge

The former 19th-century *palazzo* has been beautifully restored with fine attention to detail, faithfully preserving its unique character. The 67 elegant guest rooms and suites are individually furnished, as they would be in a private residence, with inlaid tables, antique porcelain, oil paintings and sumptuous silks and brocades, but with every modern comfort, including whirlpool baths.

The richly decorated Hostaria Bibendum, with a terrace overlooking Piazza Strozzi, presents re-interpretations of classic Italian dishes using the best ingredients with contemporary flair and imagination, complemented by the finest wines of the region.

Villa Stanley
Viale XX Settembre, 200
50019 Sesto Fiorentino,
Florence
www.charminghotels.com/villastanley

General Manager
Mr Umberto Giordano

Open all year

Rooms & Facilities
53 Rooms and Suites
Swimming pool

Rates
Single from €82 to 130
Double from €99 to 200
VAT, breakfast & service charge included

Dining
La Limonaia Restaurant & Bar

Meeting Rooms: 2
Capacity: 200 max
Package rates: on request

Credit Cards
Visa, MasterCard,
American Express, Diners

Airport
Florence Airport (FLR)
3 km/1.9 miles

Train Station
Florence Santa Maria Novella
9 km/5.6 miles

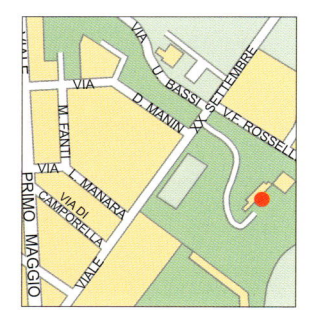

WWW.CHARMINGHOTELS.COM
+39 06 977 4591

VILLA STANLEY

Just 20 minutes from the busy centre of Florence, Villa Stanley is a peaceful, luxurious retreat set in a beautiful 14th-century building surrounded by glorious parkland to the northwest of the city.

The 25 large guest rooms, with pale-coloured walls and high painted ceilings, are elegantly furnished in early 19th-century style with polished wooden furniture and beautiful heavy silks; all with relaxing views across the gardens. There are more rooms in the restored old buildings attached to the villa's lemon grove.

The villa retains many of its interesting original architectural features, including a well and, in the grounds, the private chapel. A swimming pool has been discreetly landscaped into the immaculately planted gardens and there are also tennis courts.

The hotel's stylish restaurant, La Limonaia, has a wide choice of Tuscan and Italian specialities served either in the dining room or on the terrace overlooking the park.

SIENA

A great part of Siena's undeniable charm lies in its beautifully preserved medieval centre, but this is not a town which feels like a museum-piece: it is a busy, hard-working place, making the most of its beauty but always forward-looking.

The heart of the town is the remarkable fan-shaped Campo, scene of the famous Palio horse race. Built, like so many of the other streets, on the natural gradient of the hill on which the town stands, this has been the centre of the civic life of Siena since the 12th century, and has had many uses, including a market-place, military parade ground and sports and theatre arena.

Narrow streets wind away from the Campo which is surrounded by buildings; at the lower end is the Palazzo Pubblico, one of the finest Gothic civic buildings in Italy, with its bell tower, the Torre del Mangia, 91m tall, built in 1325. The Palazzo houses some fine paintings of the Sienese school including Simone Martini's magnificent *Maestà*, dating from 1315, and the fresco of Guidoriccio da Fogliano, captain of the Sienese army, smartly stepping out on his richly caparisoned horse. Ambrogio Lorenzetti's *Allegory of Good Government* is the largest surviving secular painting cycle from the Middle Ages.

Another of Siena's outstanding buildings is the Gothic duomo, its façade inlaid with white, red and green marble, remarkable for the richness of its sculptures, the originals of which are kept in the Museo dell'Opera.

Siena

HISTORY In the Middle Ages Siena, on the pilgrimage route between France and Rome, was under the control of the Lombards. Centuries of rivalry with Florence ended when Siena, head of the Tuscan Ghibellines and supporters of the Holy Roman Emperor, defeated the mightier Florence, supporter of the Guelphs, the papal faction, at the Battle of Montaperti in 1260. But when the son of the Holy Roman Emperor was killed at Benevento, Siena decided to side with the pope, as their support of the Ghibellines had damaged their trade in Europe. With peace came much-needed prosperity, and with it the lasting legacy of the Sienese school of painting.

Years of instability followed, though, as the town came under the control of the Visconti of Milan in the 15th century and the Habsburg emperors in the 16th. It finally came under Florence's control in 1555, after an 18-month siege.

Thankfully the Second World War had little impact on Siena, whose old centre is superbly preserved.

CULTURE Siena's Palio, which takes place twice a year, is world famous; 10 out of the 17 *contrade* or administrative wards are selected to take part and the race is watched by 30,000 people, who somehow all manage to cram into the Campo. On the day of the race the horse and jockey are blessed in the oratory of the *contrada* concerned and a colourful procession of dignitaries, flag-throwers, musicians, and the prize, the *palio* or banner, parades through the streets.

The horses and jockeys, who ride bareback, enter the Campo from the Palazzo Pubblico and line up behind a rope. A riderless horse trots up from behind and when it is level with the rope the race begins. After the inevitable false starts, the race is run three times around the Campo.

The first horse across the line, riderless or not, is the winner. Celebrations within the winning *contrada* last all night. The following day there are further parades as the winners visit the headquarters of the other *contrade*.

Food The food of Tuscany is built on the foundations of all good Mediterranean cuisine, fresh ingredients simply prepared. Tender beef from Chianina cattle, fed on Tuscan pasture, produce delicious meat for *bistecca alla fiorentina*, cooked over charcoal and served medium-rare. Bread is very good in this region and is used in many dishes including *ribollita*, a soup made of beans, cabbage and bread prepared a day in advance, then reheated the following day: *ribollita* means 'reheated'. Pork appears regularly on the menu as a main course or as sausages, salamis or dry-cured and seasoned hams.

Panforte is a rich, spiced cake of candied fruit, sprinkled with icing sugar, which was first made in the 12th century to sustain the Sienese during a siege. *Ricciarelli* are diamond-shaped biscuits made from crushed almonds. They can be bought throughout the town.

EVENTS 2nd July and 16th August: Il Palio, the world-famous horse race, consists of three laps around the Campo; it is the horse that wins, not the rider.
July–August: Siena Jazz Festival.

TRANSPORTATION The nearest airport to Siena is at Pisa. Siena's train station is 1.5km north of the centre, with regular buses into the centre (Piazza Gramsci). There are regular train and bus services from Siena to Florence, with local services to towns in the region. The historic centre of Siena is closed to cars but there is parking at the duomo and the Fortezza.

POPULATION: 55,000
AREA CODE: +39 0577
TOURIST OFFICE: +39 0577 280551
WWW.TERRESIENA.IT

Grand Hotel Continental
Via Banchi di Sopra, 85
53100 Siena
www.charminghotels.com/grandhotelcontinental

General Manager
Mr Giuseppe Artolli

Open all year

Rooms & Facilities
51 Rooms and suites
Meeting & banqueting facilities

Rates
Single from €170 to 240
Double from €190 to 435
Junior Suite from €358 to 563
Suite from €540 to 1200
VAT, breakfast & service charge not included

Dining
Sapordivino Wine Bar & Restaurant

Meeting Rooms: 3
Capacity: 150 max
Package rates: on request

Credit Cards
Visa, MasterCard, American Express, Diners

Airport
Florence Airport (FLR)
65 km/40 miles

Train Station
Siena
2 km/1.2 miles

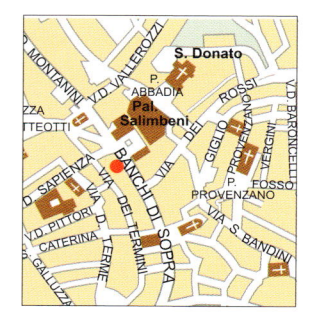

www.charminghotels.com
+39 06 977 4591

GRAND HOTEL CONTINENTAL
SIENA

GRAND HOTEL CONTINENTAL

In the historic centre of Siena, on a road which leads into the Campo, the former Palazzo Gori Pannilini, built by Pope Alexander VII for his niece, has been meticulously restored to its 17th-century splendour.

All the guest rooms have been remodelled by local craftsmen and lavishly redecorated with pale walls, rich, warm, Mediterranean-coloured fabrics and terracotta-tiled floors. Carefully chosen antiques decorate each room and some have delicate frescoes discovered after recent refurbishments, now faithfully restored.

Nabil El Sayed
Concierge

The Sapordivino wine bar and restaurant is located in the converted *palazzo* courtyard, with a beautifully glazed dome. It is ideal for lunch or dinner in an informal setting. The chef brings imagination and creativity to traditional Tuscan dishes using local ingredients including a wide choice of game. A more casual place to have an aperitif or a light snack is the Enoteca ai Banchi, the hotel's wine shop. The wine cellar is in the basement of a recently-discovered tower, its thick walls providing the perfect conditions for storing more than 500 bottles of the hotel's finest wines.

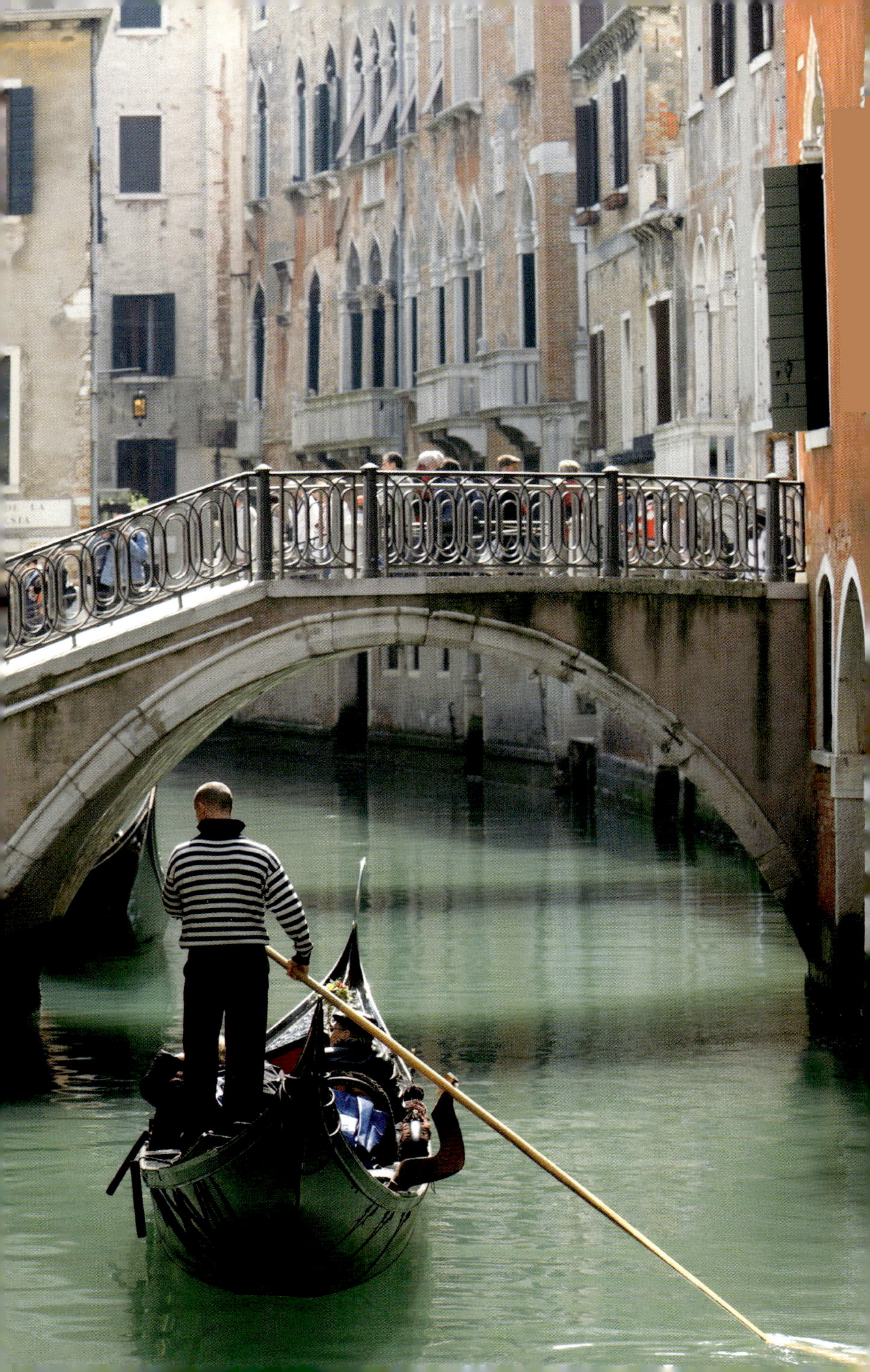

1. HOTEL EXCELSIOR p.126
2. HOTEL VILLA FRANCESCHI p.128
3. HOTEL VILLA CIPRIANI p.134
4. HOTEL VILLA MICHELANGELO p.140
5. PARK HOTEL FALORIA p.146

Veneto

The Veneto is a region rich in cultural heritage. Venice, Verona, Vicenza and Padua all warrant a day or more of exploration. The artistic and architectural achievements of these cities are unsurpassed. Tintoretto, Titian and Palladio are just a few of the brilliant artists and architects well represented in the Veneto.

VENICE & MIRA

There is nowhere quite like Venice and the Veneto. Venice was built on the reedy islets between the rivers Brenta and Piave. It eventually developed into the Serene Republic, one of the greatest maritime powers of the Middle Ages. It was an important city of trade and commerce, with the most expensive and luxurious goods of the age, particularly silks, ivory, gold and spices, being traded in the *palazzi* of the merchants along the Grand Canal.

Merchants adorned their *palazzi* and local churches with some of the most magnificent works by local artists, including the Bellini family, Titian and Giorgione. They, more than many other artists of the time, understood the unique light and luminosity of the city. These artists were followed by Veronese, Tintoretto and Canaletto, who again understood and were able to render the play of water and light to sublime effect. As a result, Venice is the richest artistic centre in northern Italy.

The merchants and rich patricians of Venice built summer villas along the Brenta Canal, at such small towns as Mira, away from the heat of the Lagoon, where the air was fresher and cooler, and where there was space to create beautiful parks and gardens.

The atmosphere of Venice today is still one of opulence and luxury; the city has plenty of stylish shops and restaurants. With its quiet backwaters lined with elegant *palazzi*, it is a city of almost unbelievable beauty.

Venice

HISTORY Founded by fugitives from the barbarian invasions of the mainland in the mid-5th century AD, its numbers swelled by refugees from the Lombard invasion of 568–69, Venice was ruled by *tribuni* appointed by the governor of Ravenna. It was later governed by a duke or *doge*, who by playing the interests of the Holy Roman Emperor against those of the Byzantine Empire, attained independence for the city in the 11th century.

As its maritime supremacy increased so too did the city's size and wealth, and having won control of the eastern Mediterranean from Genoa, Venice expanded its territory on the mainland. As the Ottoman Turks rose to power, the city's maritime influence was challenged, so the ever-pragmatic Venetians turned their attention to the mainland, and by 1420 Verona, Padua and Udine were among many mainland cities to join the Supreme Republic.

But with Turkish expansion and the increase of European power, Venice's supremacy eventually began to decline. It was conquered by Napoleon and ceded to Austria in 1797, finally becoming part of Italy in 1866.

CULTURE Venice is married to the sea. Over the centuries the sea has given Venice her power and wealth and has influenced her art and architecture. Many celebrations take place on the water: on the third Sunday in July a bridge of boats is built across the Giudecca Canal leading to the church of Redentore where Mass is celebrated to commemorate the end of a plague in the 16th century. The *Festa di San Marco e Il Bòcolo* celebrates the city's patron saint with gondola races in the Bacino. And Venice's distinctive gondolas are still very much part of the cityscape, slipping effortlessly through even the narrowest canals. You can see them being made and repaired in the Squero di San Trovaso or being cleaned and polished in any number of canal-side berths.

FOOD Some of the best cuisine of Venice and the Veneto comes from the sea. *Seppie* are cuttlefish, cooked in their own ink, served with soft *polenta*. Crab is also popular: *granseola* is spider crab, delicious served cold in its shell; *molcche* are soft-shelled crabs, fried whole. Rice is very popular in the region, and delicious creamy *risotto* served in its many varieties is often to be seen on the menu.

Perhaps Venice's most famous meat dish is *fegato alla veneziana*, thinly sliced calves' liver gently fried with onions.

Traditional wines of the area include Venice's sparkling white wine, *prosecco*, and reds and whites from the neighbouring Veneto and Friuli districts.

EVENTS Carnival is celebrated with great enthusiasm in Venice, when many people attend balls dressed in masks and elaborate costume.

Sunday after Ascension Day: *La Sensa*, symbolic ceremony recalling the traditional marriage between the Doge and the sea, with processions of gondolas and other craft.

25th April: *Festa di San Marco*: the patron saint of Venice is celebrated with gondola races from the Punta della Dogana to Sant'Elena.

July, third Sunday: *Festa del Redentore*, celebration of the ending of plague in 1576. A bridge of boats is built across the Giudecca canal over which people walk to the church of Redentore to celebrate Mass, followed by fireworks over the Lagoon.

September: *Biennale*, huge international modern art

exhibition held in alternate years (odd numbers).
September: Venice Film Festival, an annual showcase for forthcoming films, and the oldest film festival in the world.
21st November: *Festa della Madonna della Salute*, another colourful celebration to mark the end of an outbreak of plague at the church of the Salute.

Transportation

Venice's Marco Polo airport is 9km north of the city and is connected to Piazzale Roma in Venice by a fast direct bus service (30mins). You can also take a water taxi or the Alilunga boat shuttle. Trains from all over Italy terminate at Stazione Santa Lucia on the Grand Canal. Vaporetti (water buses) ply up and down the Grand Canal, and to other parts of the city.

Population: 270,000
Area code: + 39 041
Tourist office: + 39 41 529 8730
www.turismovenezia.it

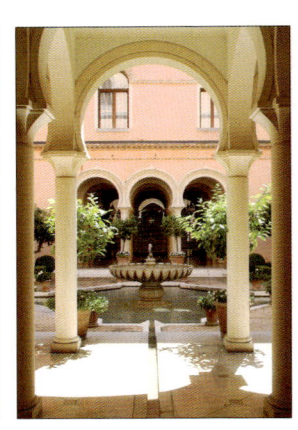

Hotel Excelsior
Lungomare Marconi, 41
30126 Venice
www.charminghotels.com/hotelexcelsior

General Manager
Mr Leone Jannuzzi

Open
April to October

Rooms & Facilities
197 Rooms and suites
Fitness centre
Private beach
Bars and restaurants
Shuttle bus to city centre

Rates
Single from €185 to 450
Double from €300 to 1020
Junior Suite from €700 to 2100
Suite from €1130 to 3800
VAT, breakfast & service charge included

Meeting Rooms: 6
Capacity: 750 max
Package rates: on request

Credit Cards
American Express, Diners, Japan Credit Bureau, MasterCard, Visa, CartaSi

Airports
Venice Marco Polo (VCE)
24 km/15 miles
Treviso Airport (TSF)
50 km/31 miles

Train Station
Venice Santa Lucia
12 km/7.5 miles

GDS CHAIN CODE: CU
AMADEUS CU VCEVEX
GALILEO CU 26243
SABRE CU 50600
WORLDSPAN CU ITVEX

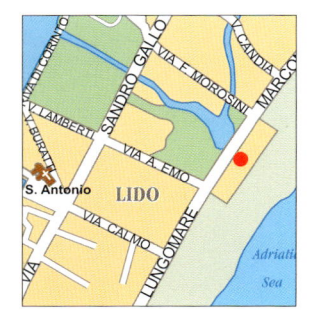

WWW.CHARMINGHOTELS.COM
+39 06 977 4591

Hotel Excelsior

Built on the Venice Lido, overlooking the Adriatic Sea and just a short boat ride from Venice itself, the imposing Excelsior is world-renowned for its grandeur and style. This magnificent looking hotel, with Moorish-style battlements and cupolas, was built in 1907 and was the first to exploit this idyllic position, away from the bustle of Venice but close enough to enjoy its many attractions.

The guest rooms, recently redecorated and refurbished, are spacious and elegant but retain the ravishing Iberian-Moorish style of the hotel's heyday, with sumptuous furnishings and intricate woodwork. All rooms have either balconies or terraces and overlook the sea, the gardens or the lagoon.

The Excelsior has several exceptional places to eat. The Tropicana Restaurant and Terrace is elegant and sophisticated; the menu comprises Italian and international cuisine with the accent on fish and seafood. This is a wonderful place to dine by candlelight, overlooking the sea. The informal Taverna Restaurant, under shady vines, serves breakfast and light lunches directly on the beach.

The hotel has a comprehensive range of amenities including a swimming pool, gym, tennis courts and water-sports.

Hotel Villa Franceschi
Via Don Minzoni, 28
30030 Venice, Mira
www.charminghotels.com/hotelvillafranceschi

General Managers
Alessandro & Dario Dal Corso

Open all year

Rooms & Facilities
25 Rooms and suites
Extensive park
Jacuzzi
Private garden
Helicopter landing
Private boat dock

Rates
Standard Single from €110 to 120
Double from €128 to 226
Junior Suite from €187 to 254
Suite from €308 to 341
VAT, breakfast & service charge included

Dining
Margherita Restaurant
Bar Palladio

Meeting Rooms: 3
Capacity: 150 max
Package rates: from €200

Credit Cards
Visa, MasterCard, American Express, Diners

Airport
Venice Marco Polo (VCE)
22 km/14 miles

Train Station
Mestre
8 km/5 miles

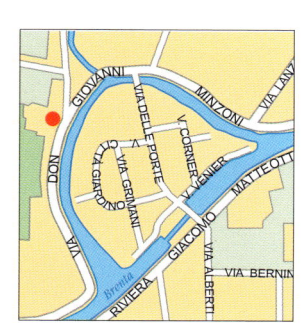

WWW.CHARMINGHOTELS.COM
+39 06 977 4591

Hotel Villa Franceschi

Situated on the banks of the meandering Brenta Canal, Hotel Villa Franceschi is a 16th-century country house set in verdant parkland, the former summer retreat of a wealthy Venetian merchant. One façade overlooks the water while the other overlooks the gardens and domestic buildings.

Villa Franceschi retains its sumptuous Venetian style: all the guest rooms are spacious with the original fireplaces and tiled floors, and are decorated with antique furniture, Murano glass chandeliers and mirrors, Carrara marbles and Rubelli fabrics. The atmosphere is one of relaxed, effortless elegance.

Alessandro & Dario Dal Corso
Owners

The older, rustic Barchessa, where boats and farm machinery were once kept, has been transformed into the reception area, bar and lounges; rooms here have direct access to the gardens.

The restaurant has a large shady veranda overlooking the gardens, The menu's focus is on traditional Venetian cuisine, with an emphasis on freshly-caught fish.

Terraces overlook the beautifully landscaped gardens, dotted with antique marble statues.

ASOLO Just 55km from Vicenza, Asolo is a delightful little town, sitting in the alpine foothills. Its location and the gentle climate attract many visitors today, as they have has done throughout the centuries. The old centre is a delightful maze of quaint arcaded streets and squares with pattering fountains and outdoor cafés.

The town is closely linked to Caterina Cornaro, Queen of Cyprus, who lived here in the 15th century. She welcomed men of learning to her court and the town has attracted many famous people down the years, including actresses, writers and poets.

The 15th century Loggia del Capitano in Piazza Maggiore has a beautiful portico and frescoed façade which dates from 1560. It now houses a local museum. The remains of Caterina Cornaro's castle, parts of which can still be visited, lie just outside the piazza. Part of the beautiful gardens were bought by Robert Browning so he could build a villa for his son, Pen.

Just a few kilometres east of Asolo, set among vineyards, is the pretty little town of Maser. Here is one of Palladio's finest buildings, the Villa Barbaro, a classic manor house with porticoed service wings to either side. Inside there are beautiful frescoes by Veronese, which incorporate architectural details in a masterly display of *trompe l'oeil* technique.

Asolo

HISTORY Originally settled in ancient times by the ancient Veneti, in the 15th century Asolo was owned by Venice, who offered it to Caterina Cornaro in exchange for the island of Cyprus, of which she was dowager queen. She accepted the offer and lived in the castle from 1489 to 1509. Her court attracted men of talent and learning, including the artist Gentile Bellini and great Renaissance scholars.

CULTURE The countryside around Asolo is one of bucolic beauty; farmhouses nestle comfortably in the rolling green countryside, with sweeping views of the surrounding hills. The town is surrounded by a number of old villas. Villa Falier has beautiful gardens. It is said the talents of Canova were discovered here when he sculpted a lion out of butter for a banquet given by Giovanni Falier.

FOOD Like the rest of the Veneto, fresh fish, locally-grown vegetables and rice form the basis of the cuisine of the region. There are some excellent farm-produced cheeses, honey, wild mushrooms, and also grappa flavoured with juniper or whortleberries. Excellent wine is produced around Conegliano and Valdobbiadene.

Events
20–29th August: Asolo Film Festival.
September: Annual Chamber Music Festival.

Transportation
The nearest airport is Venice Marco Polo airport, 63km to the east. The nearest stations are at Bassano del Grappa and Montebelluna.
By road, Asolo lies on the main SS 248 between Bassano del Grappa and Montebelluna. There are local buses around town but Asolo is a small place and can easily be explored on foot.

Population:
10,000
Area code:
+ 39 043
Tourist office:
+ 39 423 52 90 46
www.asolo.it

Hotel Villa Cipriani
Via A. Canova, 298
31011 Asolo
www.charminghotels.com/villacipriani

General Manager
Mr Leone Jannuzzi

Open all year

Rooms & Facilities
31 Rooms
Wellness space

Rates
Single from €150 to 289
Double from €205 to 580
Grand Deluxe Double from €360 to 739
VAT, breakfast & service charge included

Dining
Villa Cipriani award-winning Restaurant
Bar Il Pozzo

Meeting Rooms: 3
Capacity: 70 max
Package rates: on request

Credit Cards
American Express, Diners, MasterCard, Visa, Japan Credit Bureau, CartaSi

Airports
Venice Marco Polo (VCE)
70 km/43.5 miles
Treviso Airport (TSF)
35 km/22 miles

Train Stations
Castelfranco Veneto
15 km/9.5 miles
Bassano del Grappa
15 km/9.5 miles
Treviso
40 km/24 miles

GDS CHAIN CODE: CU
AMADEUS CU VCEVVC
GALILEO CU 58595
SABRE CU 40032
WORLDSPAN CU ITVVC

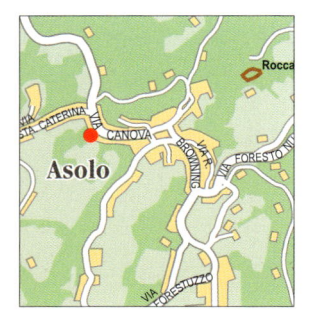

WWW.CHARMINGHOTELS.COM
+39 06 977 4591

HOTEL VILLA CIPRIANI

Towering high above the delightful medieval town of Asolo, with its charming arcaded streets and fascinating artisans' shops, this beautiful 16th-century villa, much restored and improved, was once the home of the poet Robert Browning. Surrounded by dazzling views of the Dolomites, inspirational not only to Browning but to artists such as Giorgione and Titian, the villa itself is set in well-tended terraced gardens, planted with pomegranate trees and ablaze with wild flowers.

This is a small, intimate hotel with only 31 rooms; the exposed beams, antique furniture and natural tones of cream, terracotta and greens in the décor, create an atmosphere of comfortable elegance.

Villa Cipriani also has an exceptional restaurant, renowned for the quality of its menu and the imagination and flair of its chef. Bar Il Pozzo is a delightful place for informal drinks. Breakfast is served on the terrace with its incomparable views of mountains and lush green valleys.

VICENZA is a delightful town, just 70km west of Venice, famous above all else for being the birthplace of the architect Andrea Palladio: this provincial capital has many examples of his finest buildings. It was Palladio's legacy which contributed to Vicenza being created a UNESCO world heritage site.

But Vicenza is not just a city of ston. Settled at the foot of the Colli Berici, it lies at the confluence of two rivers, the Retrone and the Bacchiglione, which brings to the town delightful vistas of water-lapped houses and quiet riverside walks. The long Corso Palladio, Vicenza's main street, is lined with magnificent *palazzi* and churches dating from the 14th–18th centuries. The Basilica is the town's most important building, dating from 1549, and it is one of the finest examples of Venetian Renaissance architecture. It was also the commission which made Palladio's name. The Teatro Olimpico, Palladio's last work, was the meeting place of the Accademia Olimpica, of which the architect was a member. Its fixed backdrop, installed by Palladio's pupil Scamozzi, is a masterpiece of *trompe l'oeil*.

But the works for which Palladio are best remembered are his villas, and these are easily visited from Vicenza. While many are now privately owned and not open to the public it is still possible to admire Palladio's mastery of proportion and elegance. Vicenza is also a good place from which to visit other towns in the Veneto, including Verona and the university town of Padua.

Vicenza

137

HISTORY Vicenza was a Roman *municipium*, and the layout of the Roman streets is still recognisable today. From the early 14th century Vicenza owed suzerainty to Scaligeri of Verona, who fortified the town against the Visconti. In the 15th century it flourished under Venetian protection. In recent years Vicenza has benefited from the rapid economic growth of much of Northern Italy.

CULTURE With its Palladian elegance it is easy to forget that Vicenza is also a thriving industrial town, the third largest exporting centre in Italy and one of the country's wealthiest cities. Steel and textile factories have moved into the eastern and western suburbs, employing tens of thousands, while twenty-five percent of Italy's exquisite gold and jewellery is manufactured here.

FOOD Like the cuisine of Venice, from which it draws its inspiration, Vicenza's food is simple, using locally-produced ingredients. Dried cod is used in *baccalà alla vicentina*, cooked in milk and served with *polenta*. The delightfully-named *Risi e bisi* is another local dish of risotto with peas. Asparagus, grapes and cherries are grown in Bassano, northeast of the city.

EVENTS 22nd January: feast of San Vincenzo, the town's patron saint. May–June: *Il Suono dell'Olimpico*, classical music concerts at the Teatro Olimpico. June–Sept: Estate Show, open-air music, theatre, dance and cinema at venues throughout the town.
8th September: feast of Our Lady of Monte Berico. Sept: Festival d'Autunno, classical theatre festival at the Teatro Olimpico.

TRANSPORTATION The nearest airports are at Venice, Verona and Milan.
Vicenza is on the main Milan–Venice rail line and most trains stop here.
Vicenza is on the main east–west autostrada, the A4 and has two exits (Vicenza Est and Vicenza Ovest). There is only limited parking in the town.

POPULATION: 120,000
AREA CODE: + 39 0444
TOURIST OFFICE: + 39 0444 320854
WWW.VICENZA.COM
TURISMO.PROVINCIA.VICENZA.IT

Hotel Villa Michelangelo

Via Sacco, 35
36057 Vicenza, Arcugnano
www.charminghotels.com/
hotelvillamichelangelo

General Manager
Mr Pietro Rusconi

Open all year

Rooms & Facilities
52 Rooms and suites
Private park
Outdoor swimming pool
Wedding and
ceremonies facilities
Golf course (18 holes) nearby

Rates
Classic Single from €90 to 170
Double from €130 to 320
Suite from €270 to 495
VAT, breakfast & service
charge included

Dining
La Loggia Restaurant

Meeting Rooms: 7
Capacity: 350 max
Package rates: on request

Credit Cards
Visa, MasterCard,
American Express,
Diners, CartaSi

Airports
Verona Airport (VRN)
56 km/35 miles
Venice Marco Polo (VCE)
76 km/47 miles

Train Station
Vicenza
7 km/4.3 miles

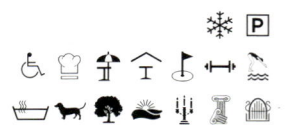

WWW.CHARMINGHOTELS.COM
+39 06 977 4591

Hotel Villa Michelangelo

Pietro Rusconi
General Manager

Set in extensive parkland and olive groves, Hotel Villa Michelangelo is an elegant, peaceful 18th-century mansion close to the centre of Vicenza. This historic city is the home town of the architect Andrea Palladio, and many examples of his work can be seen here. Vicenza is also an ideal location for visiting Venice, Padua, Verona and the Palladian villas long the Brenta Canal.

While the size of the 52 guest rooms may vary, each is individually and tastefully decorated using the finest traditional materials of the Veneto—beautiful glass, marbles and luxurious fabrics. Cool pastel-coloured walls and beamed ceilings give an old-world charm and create a comfortable atmosphere.

The restaurant, La Loggia, extends over two elegant rooms and offers indoor dining with stunning views of the Colli Berici hills. Inspired by local dishes, the chef produces traditional classic Italian cooking with a light, modern touch. Breakfast is served on the terrace overlooking the gardens.

A swimming pool is set within the villa's olive grove with a snack bar for drinks and light meals.

CORTINA D'AMPEZZO lies at 1200m, within a pleasant upland basin in the Ampezzana valley, surrounded by the peaks of the Dolomites on all sides. It has a little church with a slender narrow spire and pretty wooden tabernacle.

By the middle of the 20th century, Cortina was attracting the rich and famous for its year round skiing and the beauty of the mountains. With them came smart shops and restaurants, turning the tiny village into a prosperous little town. It is still a very attractive place to stay, offering good skiing, as well as magnificent walks, mountain biking, trekking and a wide range of other outdoor sports.

Northeast of Cortina is Lago di Misurina, one of the most stunning lakes in the Dolomites, while to the west, via a spectacular road, blasted out of the mountains by the Austrians and the beginning of the 20th century, lies Bolzano, a typically Tyrolean-looking town with Gothic architectural features.

Cortina d'Ampezzo

HISTORY Cortina was once an isolated village. It was taken by the Republic of Venice in 1420, while a century later it was conquered by the Habsburgs. Although an Austrian possession until 1920, it was never German-speaking, preserving its own dialect, Ladin. After the First World War it was given to Italy. Cortina has been attracting British visitors since the late 18th century. The 1956 Winter Olympics were held here.

CULTURE Skiing is the *raison d'être* of this attractive alpine town. The Cortina Ski School was founded in 1903 and is the oldest of its type. The area offers 100 ski slopes, covering 120km; it has 6 cable cars, 30 chair lifts and 10 cabin lifts, taking skiers to the base of Monte Cristallo at 3000m. There is also 70km of cross-country skiing as well as beautiful mountain walks and trails.

FOOD Here in the mountains the food is hearty and filling and takes on influences from Tyrolean and Venetian cuisine. Typical dishes include *casunziei*, fresh pasta stuffed with red turnip, and rich soups made of beans and local vegetables. *Smacafam* is polenta made with potatoes, mixed with cream and cooked with sausages and lard. *Fartaies* are sugar-coated deep fried pastries.

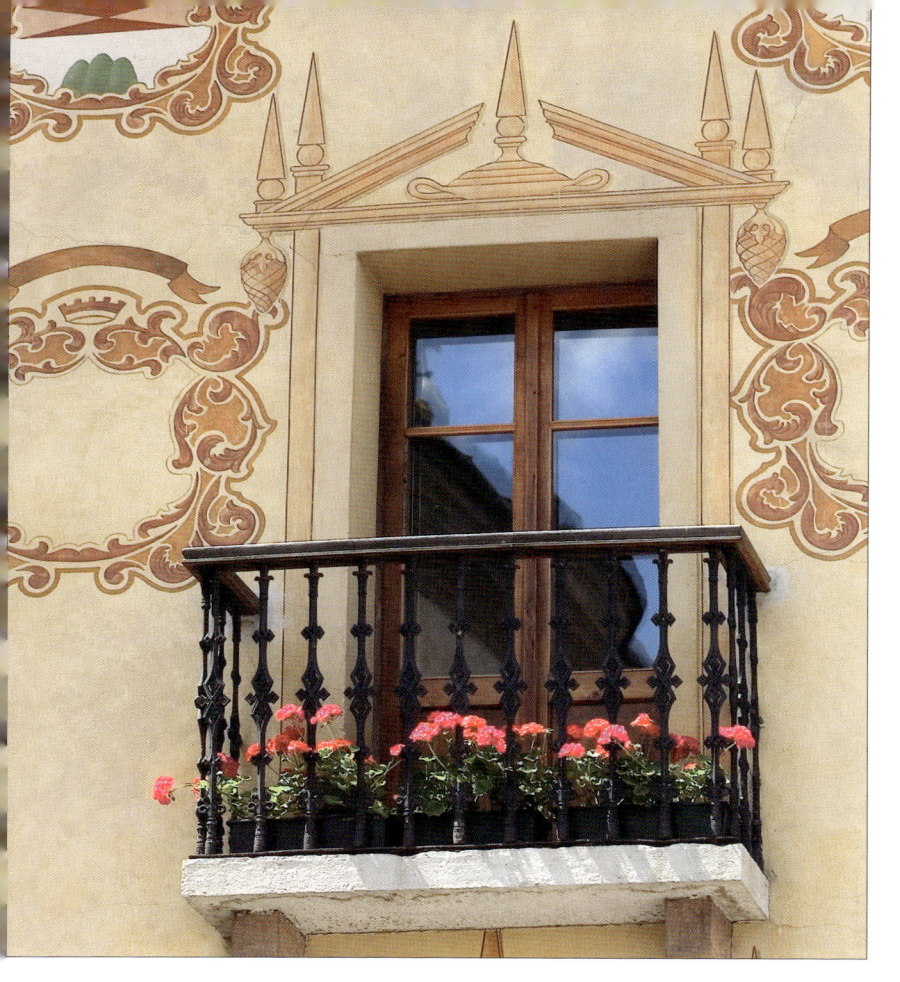

EVENTS

January: Alpine Skiing World Cup.
3rd May: St Philip and St James, patron saints' day.
14th August: fireworks and candle-lit processions.
Last week of August: *Festa de ra Bandes*, concerts and folk-dancing.
5th December: feast of St Nicholas, with processions.

TRANSPORTATION

The nearest airports are at Venice, Treviso or Verona. Trains from Venice Santa Lucia station to Calalzo di Cadore, then bus transfer to Cortina d'Ampezzo.
There are regular bus services from Mestre railway station to Cortina d'Ampezzo. Bus serices also operate from Bologna, linked to the trains from Florence, Rome and Naples.

POPULATION:
6,150
AREA CODE:
+ 39 0436
TOURIST OFFICE:
+ 39 0436 866252
www.dolomiti.org

Park Hotel Faloria
Loc. Zuel di Sopra, 46
32043 Cortina d'Ampezzo
www.charminghotels.com/parkhotelfaloria

Hotel Manager
Mrs Fabiana Rea

Open
14th June to 28th March

Rooms & Facilities
31 Rooms and suites
Restaurant and bar
Wellness centre
Fitness facilities

Rates
Double Single Use fom €105 to 240
Classic Double from €125 to 280
Suite from €160 to 720
VAT, breakfast & service charge included

Credit Cards
Visa, Mastercard, American Express, Diners, CartaSi, Eurocard, Aura, Discover Card

Airports
Venice Marco Polo (VCE)
162 km/100 miles
Treviso Airport (TSF)
133 km/82 miles

Train Station
Calalzo di Cadore
30 km/18 miles

GDS CHAIN CODE: CU
AMADEUS CU BLXPHF
GALILEO CU 38530
SABRE CU 26136
WORLDSPAN CU VCEPF

WWW.CHARMINGHOTELS.COM
+39 06 977 4591

PARK HOTEL FALORIA

Set at 1200m in the Dolomites, the charming Hotel Faloria has been welcoming guests for nearly 100 years. It is the perfect location for relaxing and exploring the surrounding mountains either on foot or by bike, while in the winter it caters to those who come to the Dolomites for the skiing. The hotel occupies two large chalet-style buildings, typical of the region, with flowers on the balconies in summer, connected by a central area with the lobby, restaurant and an informal bar.

The 31 guest rooms and suites, recently refurbished, are spacious, modern and very comfortably furnished with views over the main piazza of Moena and the surrounding mountains.

The cosy restaurant has views of the Avisio river. Using locally-sourced ingredients the menu includes classic seasonal Trentino dishes. The hotel patisserie produces delicious bread and pastries served at breakfast and in the café.

A wellness centre has been created on the top floor offering a variety of fitness programs and relaxing therapies, while enjoying magnificent views of the mountains.

Fabiana Rea
Hotel Manager

GENEVA With 40 percent of Geneva's population non-Swiss, it's not hard to understand why it is such a cosmopolitan city. It is home to the headquarters of some 200 international organisations, including the International Red Cross, which was founded in the city, and the European headquarters of the United Nations. It is also one of the most important financial centres in Europe. But business and pleasure are kept to separate sides of the city.

The old town has grown up around the Romanesque-Gothic cathedral of St Pierre, built in the 12th century. The heart of the old town is pretty Place du Bourg-de-Four, its 18th-century fountain surrounded by flowers in the summer. In Roman times it was the commercial centre of the city. In the 16th century the area was cleared and houses built for exiled Protestants, and many fine buildings of the 17th and 18th centuries survive.

Geneva has many luxury shops and interesting boutiques, the best of which are in Rue de la Croix d'Or and Rue de Rive, while a stroll down the Grand Rue is a showcase for antique shops. And of course, Geneva has a long tradition of fine watch- and clock-making and there are many jewellers. The lakefront is just a stroll from the centre. On a clear day Mont Blanc can be seen across the water. The famous Jet d'eau sends a column of water 140m into the air. On the right bank is the Brunswick Monument, with the tomb of Charles II, who left his considerable fortune to the city in return for this monument. On the right bank, in the Jardin Anglais, is the city's famous floral clock.

Geneva

History Once a border town and an important crossroads from Northern Europe to the Mediterranean, Geneva has always been at the centre of the exchange of ideas and trade. In 1387 it was granted a charter whereby it became virtually self-governing. Trade and commerce flourished and the city established itself as a good place to do business. During the Protestant Reformation of the 16th century, many victims of religious persecution fled to Geneva and John Calvin made it his base and created a Protestant Rome, which in turn did much to influence the politics, trade and administration of the city. As a result of the aristocratic and democratic in-fighting of the French Revolution, Geneva was annexed by France. The Congress of Vienna (1814–15) extended Geneva's territories, which included 16,000 Catholics whose freedom to practice their religion was guaranteed. As a city welcoming religious and economic exiles, it was perhaps only natural that Geneva should become the headquarters of so many humanitarian organisations including the International Committee of the Red Cross and the European headquarters of the United Nations.

CULTURE The culture of Geneva reflects the skills and trades of those who have made the city their home, many of them exiles. In the 17th century it grew rich on the silk trade, which flourished here thanks to the skills of the Huguenot refugees who fled here from religious persecution at home.

The city's importance as a commercial and banking centre was established in the 17th and 18th centuries, due to the development of trade during the Reformation and increased foreign investment. It was also at this time that the clock- and watch-making and gold industry flourished, along with knife- and cutlery-making of the finest quality, including many incarnations of the famous Swiss Army Knife.

Chocolate is another luxury product mastered here, with the art of chocolate-making being passed down through the generations. One of the oldest firms is Favarger, run by seven generations of the family, at Rue Chemin des Moulins. They have been making chocolate since 1826.

Food The cuisine of Geneva has an unmistakable French influence and, as is to be expected in such a cosmopolitan city, there is a wide choice of restaurants and styles of cooking. But there are plenty of traditional Swiss dishes including *fondue* and *raclette*. For an authentic *fondue*, two or three different types of cheese are melted and eaten by dipping bread into the pot. For traditional *raclette*, place a block of *raclette* cheese over an open fire, scrape away the melted cheeses and serve with boiled potatoes and pickles.

Another classic dish is *filets de perche*, a sort of Swiss fish and chips. The most genuine perch will have been caught in Lake Geneva, but they are mainly imported now: look for *filets de perche frais du lac Léman* on the menu. *Longeole* is a spicy pork sausage with wild fennel seeds, garlic and white wine.

The Canton of Geneva also produces some excellent wines, the classics using the Gamay and Chasselas grape varieties.

EVENTS Geneva hosts many annual international fairs and exhibitions. September, Thursday after the first Sunday, *Jeûne genevois,* commemoration of the date when the Huguenots in Geneva learnt of the St Bartholomew's Day massacre in Paris. 12th December: *Escalade*, a colourful re-enactment in historical costumes of the city's victory over the Savoy army in 1602.

TRANSPORTATION Geneva's airport is 5km from the city centre and has fast, regular rail and bus connections.
The best way to get around the city is on foot, as parking is very limited and expensive, but there are efficient local buses which cover the whole city.
Gare Cornavin is the central railway station in Geneva, with connections to other Swiss towns and cities.

POPULATION: 190,000
AREA CODE: + 41 22
TOURIST OFFICE: + 41 22 909 70 00
WWW.GENEVE-TOURISME.CH

Hotel Bristol
10, Rue du Mont-Blanc
1201 Geneva
www.charminghotels.com/hotelbristol

Executive Director
Mr Manuel Pedro Marmelo

Open all year

Rooms & Facilities
100 Rooms and suites
Piano bar

Rates
Single from CHF 360 to 635 (€248 to 437)
Double from CHF 495 to 680 (€341 to 468)
Junior suite and Duplex CHF 1010 (€695)
Suite from CHF 2100 to 2600 (€1446 to 1790)
WI-FI, entry to wellness centre, VAT & service charge included
Breakfast not included

Dining
Le Relais Bristol Restaurant

Meeting Rooms: 6
Capacity: 200 max
Package rates: on request

Credit Cards
Visa, MasterCard, American Express, Diners, JCB

Airport
Geneva Airport (GVA)
5 km/3.1 miles

Train Station
Cornavin
0.3 km/0.18 miles

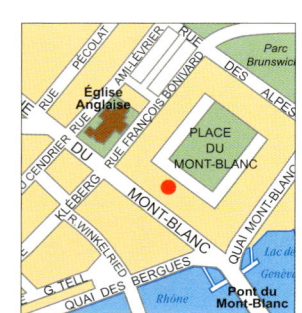

WWW.CHARMINGHOTELS.COM
+39 06 977 4591

HOTEL BRISTOL

Overlooking a quiet garden near the historic centre, and just a few steps from Lake Geneva, the Bristol is a gracious traditional European-style hotel exuding old-world charm in the heart of the city. It is ideally located for all the main tourist sites and the city's most fashionable shopping streets.

Behind the modern-looking façade, the 100 guest rooms are spacious, welcoming and classically elegant, decorated with antiques specially selected to blend in and to complement the hotel's modern design. There are views of the Mont-Blanc Square or across to Geneva's bustling centre.

Béatrice Vaisseau
Reservations Manager

Relais Bristol is the hotel's distinguished and award-winning restaurant, offering sophisticated seasonal Mediterranean cuisine. The chef takes pride in creating innovative dishes combining local produce with intriguing Mediterranean flavours. Drinks, aperitifs, digestifs and cocktails are available in the relaxing informal Piano Bar.

The Bristol Wellness Centre offers a state-of-the-art gym and massage cabin, while bio sauna, Finnish sauna, steam room and light therapy are available at the spa centre.

ISTANBUL The various incarnations of this vibrant city—Byzantium, Constantinople and Istanbul—reflect the different civilizations and customs which have influenced it. Often described as a cross-roads where East meets West, the Gateway to Asia, it is a city with extraordinary layers of culture, at the same time both familiar and exotic. With its population of 13 million, it is also one of the world's megacities, and is the financial, economic and cultural centre of Turkey even though it is not the capital. Stretching along both sides of the Bosphorus, Istanbul is the only city in the world positioned astride two continents.

Istanbul is a beguiling city, overlooking the Bosphorus and encompassing the natural harbour of the Golden Horn. Its skyline of domes and minarets is unmistakable. There are countless mosques to visit; among the most breathtaking is the colossal Haghia Sophia, the largest cathedral in the world for over 1,000 years, built as a church in 306 and converted into a mosque in the mid-15th century. With its massive dome, it is considered to be the highpoint of Byzantine architecture and a model for other buildings the world over.

Istanbul is also justly famous for its bazaars, filled with bargain-hunters and hagglers and with a dazzling array of goods from brass to spices. The amazing Topkapı Palace gives an insight into the extravagant lives of the Ottoman sultans.

Istanbul

HISTORY Byzantium was settled on the European side of the Bosphorus in 667 BC by the Greek king Byzas. It was besieged and damaged in AD 196 by the Romans, but was quick to recover its former prosperity. It came to Constantine's attention in 324 and became the capital of his Roman Empire in 330, and was renamed Constantinople. It became the centre of diplomacy, culture and commerce, as well as the centre of Greek Orthodox Christianity, one of the most important cities of the Christian world. Sacked during the Fourth Crusade in 1204, its fortunes steadily declined until it was finally taken, in 1453, by the Ottoman sultan, Mehmet the Conqueror, who made it the capital of the Ottoman Empire. He immediately set about restoring and improving the city. Further artistic and architectural accomplishments came under the rule of Süleyman the Magnificent (1520–66), with the help of his court architect Sinan. Westernisation of Istanbul started in the 18th century as the influence of European cities became greater. Turkey was created a republic in 1923 under Kemal Ataürk.

CULTURE Istanbul has been influenced and shaped by many cultures, and one of the most magical manifestations of these is the Yerebatan Saraı, the sunken palace or cistern, one of hundreds built underneath the city to conserve fresh water. It was built in the 6th century, in the days of Emperor Justinian I, who also built the basilica of Haghia Sophia, dedicated to the Holy Wisdom.

Five hundred metres from the church, below street level, the cistern is an atmospherically-lit forest of 336 columns within a space 140m long, 70m wide. Walking above the water on wooden pathways, fish swim beneath your feet while gorgons' heads, the snake-headed capitals of the columns, gaze at you from beneath the water.

FOOD There is (almost) nothing to compare with eating freshly-caught fish, grilled on the boat on which it was caught, served in a tasty sandwich on the dockside, overlooking the skipping ferries on the Bosphorus. Istanbul has perfected the art of street food, with delicious grilled meat (kebabs) at almost every street corner. Istanbul cuisine has been influenced over the centuries by the culinary traditions of Asia, the Middle East and the Mediterranean, fragranced with the herbs and spices which have been traded through the bazaars of the city for millennia.

Key ingredients include fresh vegetables: onion, garlic, lentils, beans, tomatoes, aubergine and green pepper, flavoured with spices and herbs, especially cumin, oregano, thyme, paprika and black pepper. Fruit such as dates, apricots, figs, apples and grapes are all important ingredients in Turkish cuisine.

Events

11th August–9th September: Ramadan, a 30-day period of fasting during the daylight hours and prayer, followed by three days of feasting and celebration.

30th August: Victory Day, national holiday.

29th October: celebration of the founding of the republic.

Transportation

Istanbul's Atatürk Airport is about 25km from the city centre (Taksim Square) and is connected by shuttle bus. Istanbul has an extensive but confusing public transport system, but exploring the old city is best done on foot. If you do want to use public transport, buy a Smart Ticket (AKBIL) which can be used on buses, trams, metro and ferries. There is a large fleet of municipal and privately-run buses which criss-cross the city. There is also an efficient tram service. There are two underground funicular railways.

Ferry boats zip across the Bosphorus from the European side of the city to the Asian. There are plenty of taxis, but be sure to know how much your journey will be before you get in the cab.

Population:
13 million
Area code:
+ 90 212 (European side)
+ 90 216 (Asian side)
Tourist office:
+ 90 212 522 4902
+ 90 212 511 5888
www.tourismturkey.org

Sirkeci Konak
Taya Hatun Sokak, 5
34120 Sirkeci-Istanbul
www.charminghotels.com/sirkecikonak

General Manager
Mr Faruk Boyacı

Open all year

Rooms & Facilities
54 Rooms
Indoor swimming pool
Turkish bath
Sauna, fitness centre

Rates
Single from €146 to 160
Standard Double from €184 to 200
Superior Double from €240 to 255
Deluxe Double from €310 to 325
VAT, breakfast & service Charge included

Dining
Neyzade Restaurant (traditional Ottoman cuisine)
Sirkeci Balıkçısı (seafood restaurant)

Meeting Rooms: 2
Capacity: 35 max
Rates: on request

Credit Cards
Visa, MasterCard, American Express

Airports
Istanbul Atatürk (IST)
20 km/13 miles
Istanbul Sabiha Gökçen (SAW)
60 km/37 miles

Train Station
Sirkeci
0.2 km/0.12 miles

GDS CHAIN CODE: CU
AMADEUS CU ISTIRK
GALILEO CU 66782
SABRE CU 79656
WORLDSPAN CU SIRK

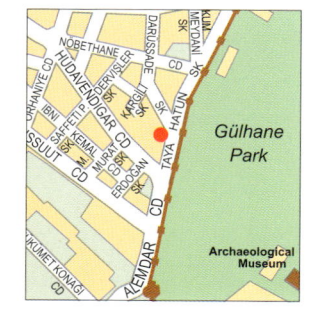

WWW.CHARMINGHOTELS.COM
+39 06 977 4591

SIRKECI KONAK

This exceptionally welcoming hotel is ideally positioned in the heart of the Istanbul's historic centre, an ideal location from which to explore 2,000 years of history and just minutes away from the Topkapı Palace, the magnificent Blue Mosque and Haghia Sophia.

Though a modern hotel it effortlessly combines the opulent 19th-century style of an Ottoman *konak* or mansion with 21st-century comfort and convenience. The rooms are beautifully decorated in neutral tones with wooden floors and colourful Turkish carpets; some rooms have views across neighbouring Gülhane Park.

Farouk Boyaci
General Manager

The Neyzade Restaurant, with a terrace and stunning views across to the Bosphorus, has an interesting menu of traditional Anatolian dishes, while the Sirkeci Balıkçısı serves fresh fish landed daily at the harbour.

Naturally, the hotel offers a hamam, where you can relax and experience a traditional Turkish steam-bath and massage. There is also a swimming pool, sauna and fitness centre as well. It is also possible to learn how to cook authentic Turkish dishes in the hotel kitchen.

KYOTO Situated in the centre of Honshu island, Kyoto is truly at the heart of Japan. Once the imperial capital, it is now a busy modern commercial and academic centre. The main industries based here are IT and electronics, and there are more than 35 universities, colleges and places of higher education and research.

But Kyoto is much visited by tourists for its natural beauty and its cultural heritage, which spans its 1,200 years as the imperial first city. There are more than 2,000 Buddhist temples and Shinto shrines, countless palaces and beautiful gardens, all in an amazing state of preservation thanks to Kyoto being spared the firebombing of the Second World War. The historic monuments of ancient Kyoto were designated a UNESCO World Heritage Site in 1994.

Kyoto is an exciting mixture of the modern and the traditional and the city manages to preserve successfully much of its old-style housing and streets alongside ultra-modern office blocks and developments. The city has also done much to ensure the survival and continuation of many of the traditional crafts which have evolved over the passing years, so today the artists of Kyoto create exquisite hand-crafted objects to traditional designs and methods.

Japanese artistic sensibility and love of nature unite to perfection in Kyoto's superb gardens, where, thanks to the region's seasonable climate, luxuriant vegetation and delicate flowers have been landscaped with an unerring eye for detail to create perfect vistas.

Kyoto

HISTORY The Emperor moved his court here in the 8th century, away from the powerful Buddhist clergy who were becoming increasingly involved in the affairs of state. Kyoto became capital in the 11th century, and remained so until 1868, when it was transferred to Edo (Tokyo).

For most of the time, the Imperial capital was peaceful; the worst period of unrest came in the mid-15th century, during the Onin War, when battles between feuding *samurai* factions broke out, eventually drawing in the court nobility as well as religious splinter groups. The nobles' already impressive mansions were heavily fortified. Streets were dug up to prevent the spread of fires and defences were thrown up, but still many buildings were destroyed.

During the Second World War, Kyoto was considered by the United States as a possible target for the atom bomb, but the city was spared because of its historical significance. The result today is that Kyoto, more than most other Japanese cities, has a wealth of pre-war buildings, including *machiya*, the traditional Japanese wooden town houses.

CULTURE There are many different facets to Japanese culture, some of which can be experienced first-hand. *Chado*, or *sado*, is the traditional Japanese tea ceremony where powdered green tea is prepared with great care and ritual, mixing it with hot water using a bamboo whisk. It is finally served with great dignity to honoured guests.

Calligraphy, or *shodo*, was introduced to Japan from China in the 6th century as a means of keeping records. Once an essential skill using brushes and ink, it is now one of the many traditional Japanese handicrafts which are nurtured within the city.

Flower-arranging, or *kado*, is a well-known craft; it originated in Japan in ancient times when flowers were arranged as offerings in the temples and shrines. In the 15th century, as domestic architectural styles changed, it became the custom to arrange flowers within an alcove or niche to enhance the size and proportion of a room. Japanese flower arrangements are designed to accentuate the beauty of flowers and plants in their natural state.

Food Being far from the sea, Kyoto has developed a wide range of imaginative vegetable-based dishes, many unique to the city. Japan as a whole has an incredible choice of styles of food. *Sushi* is a now a world-wide cuisine and is perhaps the most characteristic of all Japanese cooking. It was originally a way of preserving salted fish by fermenting it in rice. It is a healthy cuisine, combining fresh, seasonal vegetables, mushrooms, seafood and meat with rice flavoured with vinegar, and can be eaten raw, cooked or marinated.

Kaiseki-ryori is an art in its own right, a multi-course, highly sophisticated and artistic culinary experience. Only the freshest seasonal ingredients are used, being seasoned and cooked to enhance the naturalness of their taste and texture. The dishes are meticulously served on plates specially chosen to enhance the appearance; dishes are often garnished with leaves and flowers.

Shojin–roi is eaten mainly by Buddhists as it prohibits the use of meat, fish, and all root vegetables, as to harvest them would mean killing the whole plant.

EVENTS 15th May: *Aoi Matsuri,* festival at the two Kamo shrines to the north of the city. Procession of 500 participants from the Imperial Palace to the temples dressed in ceremonial court costumes to pray for a good harvest. July: *Gion Matsuri,* one of the three iconic festivals of Kyoto. Parade of floats decorated with ancient tapestries. 22nd October: *Jidai Matsuri,* one of the largest festivals in Kyoto.

TRANSPORTATION
Kyoto does not have its own airport, the nearest are Kansai or Osaka, with frequent, fast links to Kyoto railway station. There is an efficient and extensive bus network, with announcements in English and signs in the Latin alphabet.
Kyoto has two underground lines. Kyoto railway station has frequent services, many by Bullet Train.

POPULATION:
1,500,00
AREA CODE:
+ 81 75
TOURIST OFFICE:
+ 81 075 343 0548
WWW.KYOTO.TRAVEL

Hotel Granvia Kyoto
901 Higashi-shiokoji-cho,
Shiokoji-Sagaru
Karasuma-dori, Shimogyo-ku
600-8216 Kyoto
www.charminghotels.com/
hotelgranviakyoto

General Manager
Mr Hiroyuki Sakamoto

Open all year

Rooms & Facilities
535 Rooms and suites
Exclusive Granvia Floor with
private lounge
13 banqueting rooms
Fitness facilities and shops
WI-FI access in all the meeting rooms

Rates
Single/Double from
JPY 26,000 to 40,000
(from €161 to 248)
Suite from
JPY 60,000 to 400,000
(from €372 to 2,481)
VAT, breakfast & service
charge not included

Dining
13 Restaurants with
international cuisine

Meeting Rooms: 13
Capacity: 1,400 max

Airports
Kansai Airport (KIX)
97 km/60 miles

Train Station
Kyoto Station on site

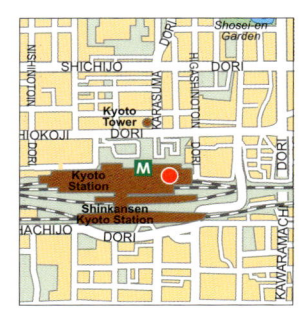

www.charminghotels.com
+39 06 977 4591

Hotel Granvia Kyoto

This is an exclusive deluxe hotel within the JR Kyoto Station with easy access to the airport and other major centres such as Osaka and Tokyo. Also within this building are a museum, a department store, and shops and restaurants.

The 535 guest rooms and suites are spread over the 7th to 15th floors of this spectacular building, with amazing views across the Kyoto skyline. All the guest rooms are tastefully decorated, combining modern, contemporary design with the traditional. This is a theme explored by the hotel's incredible art collection which, through more than 1,000 paintings, sculptures, photographs and installations by some of Japan's most famous artists, looks at the contrast of modern and traditional art.

The hotel has an amazing choice of restaurants, including a sushi bar, a traditional teahouse dining room, many restaurants serving either ultra-modern or traditional Japanese cuisine, a French bistro and an Italian eatery. There are also three comfortable bars for drinks and light meals.

Hiroyuki Sakamoto
General Manager

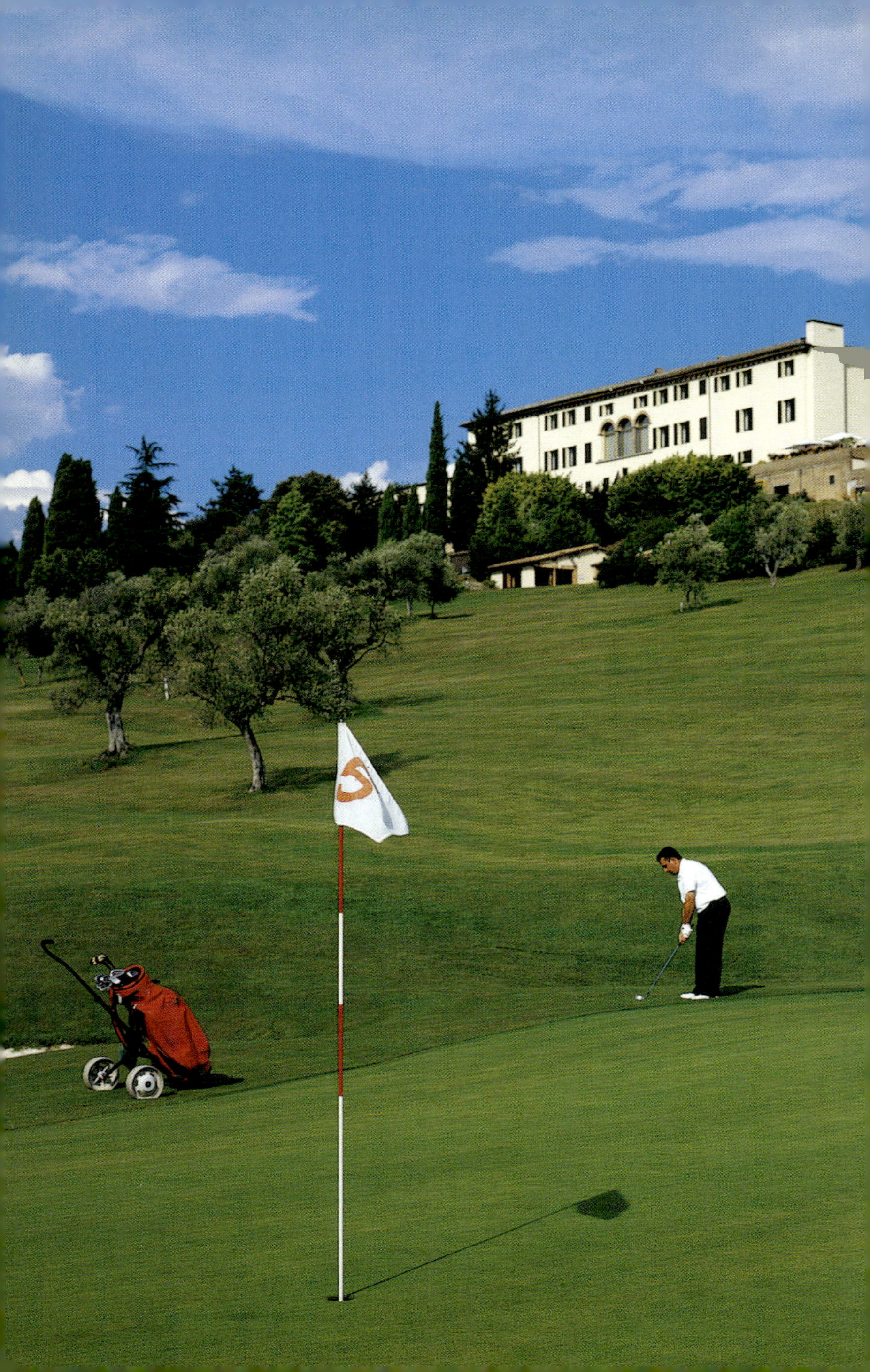

AMENITIES

ITALY	SPA SERVICES	FITNESS FACILITIES	GOLF	TENNIS	CHILDREN'S ACTIVITIES	MEETING FACILITIES	PAGE NO.
CAPRI HOTEL LA FLORIDIANA	♦	♦		♦			16
ISCHIA HOTEL MIRAMARE E CASTELLO	♦	♦				♦	22
RIMINI NATIONAL HOTEL	♦	♦	♦		♦	♦	36
ROME HOTEL D'INGHILTERRA						♦	46
ROME RESIDENZA DI RIPETTA						♦	50
ROME HOTEL VILLA MORGAGNI		♦				♦	56
GARDONE RIVIERA HOTEL VILLA DEL SOGNO	♦	♦		♦		♦	64
CASTELLANETA MARINA ALBOREA ECO LODGE	♦	♦	♦	♦	♦	♦	72
CASTELLANETA MARINA GRAND HOTEL KALIDRIA	♦	♦	♦	♦	♦	♦	74
CALA CAPRA HOTEL CAPO D'ORSO	♦	♦		♦	♦	♦	82
SANTA TERESA GALLURA VALLE DELL'ERICA RESORT THALASSO & SPA	♦	♦	♦		♦		88
FAVIGNANA CAVE BIANCHE HOTEL		♦					96
FLORENCE HOTEL HELVETIA & BRISTOL						♦	106
FLORENCE, SESTO FIORENTINO VILLA STANLEY		♦		♦		♦	108
SIENA GRAND HOTEL CONTINENTAL						♦	116
VENICE HOTEL EXCELSIOR	♦		♦	♦	♦	♦	126
VENICE, MIRA HOTEL VILLA FRANCESCHI	♦	♦	♦	♦	♦	♦	128
ASOLO VILLA CIPRIANI	♦	♦		♦		♦	134
VICENZA, ARCUGNANO HOTEL VILLA MICHELANGELO		♦	♦			♦	140
CORTINA D'AMPEZZO PARK HOTEL FALORIA	♦	♦	♦	♦	♦		146

SWITZERLAND

GENEVA HOTEL BRISTOL	♦	♦				♦	154

TURKEY

ISTANBUL SIRKECI KONAK	♦	♦				♦	162

JAPAN

KYOTO HOTEL GRANVIA KYOTO		♦				♦	170

SPA SERVICES

ITALY	BODY THERAPIES	MASSAGE	SKIN CARE	HAIR SALON	AESTHETICS	PRIVATE SPA ROOM	COUPLE'S ROOM	TREATMENT ROOMS
CAPRI HOTEL LA FLORIDIANA		♦						
Pantarei Beauty Farm 600m. Shiatsu corner massage								
ISCHIA HOTEL MIRAMARE E CASTELLO	♦	♦			♦	♦		♦
RIMINI NATIONAL HOTEL	♦	♦	♦		♦	♦	♦	♦
GARDONE RIVIERA HOTEL VILLA DEL SOGNO	♦	♦	♦			♦		
CASTELLANETA MARINA ALBOREA ECO LODGE	♦	♦	♦	♦	♦	♦	♦	♦
CASTELLANETA MARINA GRAND HOTEL KALIDRIA	♦	♦	♦		♦	♦	♦	♦
CALA CAPRA HOTEL CAPO D'ORSO	♦	♦	♦		♦			♦
SANTA TERESA GALLURA VALLE DELL'ERICA RESORT THALASSO & SPA	♦	♦	♦		♦	♦	♦	♦
VENICE HOTEL EXCELSIOR		♦						
VENICE, MIRA HOTEL VILLA FRANCESCHI								
Nearby								
ASOLO VILLA CIPRIANI	♦	♦						
CORTINA D'AMPEZZO PARK HOTEL FALORIA	♦	♦	♦		♦	♦		♦
Hair salon nearby								
SWITZERLAND								
GENEVA HOTEL BRISTOL		♦						
Wellness Centre								
TURKEY								
ISTANBUL SIRKECI KONAK		♦						

FITNESS FACILITIES

ITALY	POOL	WHIRL-POOL	SAUNA	STEAM ROOM	CERTIFIED TRAINERS	STUDIO CLASSES	HOURS OF OPERATION
CAPRI HOTEL LA FLORIDIANA	Fitness centre 500m						
ISCHIA HOTEL MIRAMARE E CASTELLO	●○		✦		✦		8am–8pm
RIMINI NATIONAL HOTEL	○	○	●	●			
ROME HOTEL VILLA MORGAGNI			✦				
CASTELLANETA MARINA ALBOREA ECO LODGE	✦	✦	✦	✦	✦	✦	9am–7pm
CASTELLANETA MARINA GRAND HOTEL KALIDRIA	✦	✦	✦	✦	✦	✦	9am–7pm
CALA CAPRA HOTEL CAPO D'ORSO	✦	✦		✦		✦	9am–1pm 4pm–8pm
	Aquagym, jetstreams, hamam, yoga stretching						
SANTA TERESA GALLURA VALLE DELL'ERICA RESORT THALASSO & SPA	✦	✦	✦	✦	✦	✦	9am–1pm 3pm–7pm
FAVIGNANA CAVE BIANCHE HOTEL	○						
FLORENCE, SESTO FIORENTINO VILLA STANLEY	✦						
VENICE, MIRA HOTEL VILLA FRANCESCHI	Fitness facilities						
ASOLO VILLA CIPRIANI			✦	✦			10am–7pm
VICENZA, ARCUGNANO HOTEL VILLA MICHELANGELO	○						
CORTINA D'AMPEZZO PARK HOTEL FALORIA	●	✦	●	●	✦		10am–8pm
SWITZERLAND							
GENEVA HOTEL BRISTOL		✦	✦	✦			7.30am–9.30pm
TURKEY							
ISTANBUL SIRKECI KONAK	✦		✦				12am–10pm
JAPAN							
KYOTO HOTEL GRANVIA KYOTO	✦	✦		✦			9am–7pm

○ outdoor ● indoor

GOLF

ITALY	COURSE NAME	ON-SITE	FEES	PAR	YARDAGE	RATING	SLOPE	DESIGNER
RIMINI NATIONAL HOTEL	Rimini Golf Club	10 km		18				Jim Fazio
GARDONE RIVIERA HOTEL VILLA DEL SOGNO	Bogliaco	6 km		70	5298			
	Gardagolf	12 km		72	5870			
CASTELLANETA MARINA ALBOREA ECO LODGE	Riva dei Tessali Golf Club Castellaneta	7 km		71	5947			John D. Harris and Associated Italian Office Arch. Marco Croze
CASTELLANETA MARINA GRAND HOTEL KALIDRIA	Riva dei Tessali Golf Club Castellaneta	7 km		71	5947			John D. Harris and Associated Italian Office Arch. Marco Croze
CALA CAPRA HOTEL CAPO D'ORSO	Capo d'Orso Pitch & Putt 9 Holes	♦	May/Ju-Se € 40 Jul/Aug €56	27	645m Hotel guests only: reduction 50%			
SANTA TERESA GALLURA VALLE DELL'ERICA RESORT THALASSO & SPA	Erica Golf Pitch & Putt Putt & Putt 18 Holes	♦						
VENICE HOTEL EXCELSIOR	Venice Golf Course - Alberoni	15 min.		72	6039 m			Cruikshank & C.K. Cotton
VENICE, MIRA HOTEL VILLA FRANCESCHI	Golf Club Frassanelle	20 km						
ASOLO VILLA CIPRIANI	Asolo Golf Club	12 km		72	6283 m			Stan Eby
VICENZA, ARCUGNANO HOTEL VILLA MICHELANGELO	Golf Club Colli Berici	12 km Hotel guest reduction		71	5798 m			
CORTINA D'AMPEZZO PARK HOTEL FALORIA	Nearby							

TENNIS

ITALY	No. OF COURTS	No. COURTS FOR NIGHT PLAY	No. OF INDOOR COURTS	PRO SHOP	STRINGING	SURFACE
CAPRI HOTEL LA FLORIDIANA						
	Tennis club nearby 300m					
GARDONE RIVIERA HOTEL VILLA DEL SOGNO	1	–	–	–	–	Synthetic green
CASTELLANETA MARINA ALBOREA ECO LODGE	10	10	2	–	–	Clay and hardcourt
CASTELLANETA MARINA GRAND HOTEL KALIDRIA	10	10	2	–	–	Clay and hardcourt
CALA CAPRA HOTEL CAPO D'ORSO	1	–	–	–	–	
FLORENCE, SESTO FIORENTINO VILLA STANLEY	1	1	–	–	–	
VENICE HOTEL EXCELSIOR	–	–	–	–	–	
	Nearby					
VENICE, MIRA HOTEL VILLA FRANCESCHI	–	–	–	–	–	
	Nearby					
ASOLO VILLA CIPRIANI	–	–	–	–	–	
	Nearby 5km					
CORTINA D'AMPEZZO PARK HOTEL FALORIA	–	–	–	–	–	
	Nearby					

CHILDREN'S ACTIVITIES

ITALY	AGE GROUP (YRS)	TIME PERIOD	KID'S POOL	PLAYGROUND	HOURS OF OPERATION
RIMINI NATIONAL HOTEL	3–15	June–Sept		◆	12.30am–3.30pm
CASTELLANETA MARINA ALBOREA ECO LODGE	3–8				3pm–10pm
CASTELLANETA MARINA GRAND HOTEL KALIDRIA	3–8				3pm–10pm
SANTA TERESA GALLURA VALLE DELL'ERICA RESORT THALASSO & SPA	3–12	May–Sept	◆	◆	9am–11pm
VENICE HOTEL EXCELSIOR	0–12	June–August	◆	◆	9am–6pm
VENICE, MIRA HOTEL VILLA FRANCESCHI	Children's facilities				
CORTINA D'AMPEZZO PARK HOTEL FALORIA			◆		

MEETING FACILITIES

	No. OF MEETING ROOMS	AUDITORIUM SEATS MAXIMUM	CLASSROOM SEATS MAXIMUM	COCKTAIL/ RECEPTION MAXIMUM	BANQUET/ RECEPTION MAXIMUM	BOARDROOM SEATS MAXIMUM
ITALY						
ISCHIA HOTEL MIRAMARE E CASTELLO	1	–	30	80	80	30
RIMINI NATIONAL HOTEL	5	250	100	300	300	–
ROME HOTEL D'INGHILTERRA	2	60	30	100	80	27
ROME RESIDENZA DI RIPETTA	6	220	80	200	180	68
ROME HOTEL VILLA MORGAGNI	1	50	18	60	60	22
GARDONE RIVIERA HOTEL VILLA DEL SOGNO	1	30	–	–	–	–
CASTELLANETA MARINA ALBOREA ECO LODGE	30	600	200	650	420	80
CASTELLANETA MARINA GRAND HOTEL KALIDRIA	30	600	200	650	420	80
CALA CAPRA HOTEL CAPO D'ORSO	1	150	40	150	–	80
FLORENCE HOTEL HELVETIA & BRISTOL	4	80	50	100	60	30
FLORENCE, SESTO FIORENTINO VILLA STANLEY	2	90	90	200	120	–
SIENA GRAND HOTEL CONTINENTAL	3	110	40	150	110	35
VENICE HOTEL EXCELSIOR	6	500	240	750	400	75
VENICE, MIRA HOTEL VILLA FRANCESCHI	5	180	90	150	180	80
ASOLO VILLA CIPRIANI	3	50	50	70	70	–
VICENZA, ARCUGNANO HOTEL VILLA MICHELANGELO	7	300	180	350	300	40
SWITZERLAND						
GENEVA HOTEL BRISTOL	6	120	50	150	90	45
TURKEY						
ISTANBUL SIRKECI KONAK	2	40	30	50	40	–
JAPAN						
KYOTO HOTEL GRANVIA KYOTO	13	2800	1800	2300	1200	–

CHARMING HOTELS GDS CU CODES
FOR TRAVEL AGENTS ONLY

ITALY	Sabre	Worldspan	Amadeus	Galileo
CAPRI HOTEL LA FLORIDIANA	*	*	*	*
ISCHIA HOTEL MIRAMARE E CASTELLO	*	*	*	*
SORRENTO LA TONNARELLA	CU 53203	CU RROLT	CU RROLTS	CU 79889
RIMINI NATIONAL HOTEL	CU 58738	CU NATI	CU RMIATI	CU 74168
ROME HOTEL D'INGHILTERRA	CU 28263	CU 3993	CU ROMDIN	CU 43306
ROME HOTEL HOMS	CU 64417	CU ROM61	CU ROMH61	CU 51370
ROME RESIDENZA DI RIPETTA	CU 7573	CU ROMRR	CU ROMRRS	CU 73423
ROME HOTEL SOLE AL PANTHEON	CU 9364	CU SOLE	CU ROMSOL	CU 26784
ROME RESIDENZA TORRE COLONNA	*	*	*	*
ROME HOTEL VILLA MORGAGNI	CU 34331	CU ROM69	CU ROMH69	CU 54585
GARDONE RIVIERA HOTEL VILLA DEL SOGNO	CU 5428	CU SOGN	CU VRNOGN	CU 50736
CASTELLANETA MARINA ALBOREA ECO LODGE	*	*	*	*
CASTELLANETA MARINA GRAND HOTEL KALIDRIA	CU 62066	CU BRIKA	CU BRIKAL	CU 6216
CALA CAPRA HOTEL CAPO D'ORSO	CU 34701	CU ORSO	CU OLBRSO	CU 57297
SANTA TERESA GALLURA VALLE DELL'ERICA RESORT THALASSO & SPA	CU 51138	CU OLBER	CU OLBRIC	CU 39508
FAVIGNANA CAVE BIANCHE HOTEL	CU 44578	CU EGAD	CU TPSGAD	CU 72406
FLORENCE HOTEL HELVETIA & BRISTOL	*	*	*	*
FLORENCE, SESTO FIORENTINO VILLA STANLEY	*	*	*	*
SIENA GRAND HOTEL CONTINENTAL	*	*	*	*
VENICE HOTEL EXCELSIOR	CU 50600	CU ITVEX	CU VCEVEX	CU 26243
VENICE, MIRA HOTEL VILLA FRANCESCHI	*	*	*	*
ASOLO HOTEL VILLA CIPRIANI	CU 40032	CU ITVVC	CU VCEVVC	CU 58595
VICENZA, ARCUGNANO HOTEL VILLA MICHELANGELO	*	*	*	*
CORTINA D'AMPEZZO PARK HOTEL FALORIA	CU 26136	CU VCEPF	CU BLXPHF	CU 38530

* Codes managed by other organizations. For online reservations, see www.charminghotels.com

SWITZERLAND	Sabre	Worldspan	Amadeus	Galileo
GENEVA HOTEL BRISTOL	*	*	*	*
TURKEY				
ISTANBUL SIRKECI KONAK	CU 79656	CU SIRK	CU ISTIRK	CU 66782
JAPAN				
KYOTO HOTEL GRANVIA KYOTO	*	*	*	*

PHOTO CREDITS

All hotel images have been provided by the hotels themselves. Other imgages as follows:

Cover: Alison Shaw/Corbis/Red Dot

©istockphoto.com: p.10 /chaoss; p. 12 /karambol; pp.18, 79 /pacaypalla; p.24 /Flory; p.25 /nicalfc; p.26 /Derona; p.27 /Angelafoto; pp.30, 34, 66, 143 /anzeletti; p.32 /vspn24; p.35 /tovstiadi; p.38 /juuce; p.40 /Matthew71; pp. 42, 43, 45, 123 /compassandcamera; p.44 /goldhafen; pp.58, 60, 142 /AlbertoSimonetti; p.61 /messenjah; p.62 /LuigiConsiglio; p.63 /clayhouse; p.68 /jojobob; p.70 /lucamanieri; pp.76, 78 /seraficus; p.80 /flodiver; p.81 /crazy82; p.84 /rotofrank; p.98 /javarman3; pp.100, 114 /miralex; p.101 /Alysta; p. 102 /timurka; p.104 /carolgaranda; p.110 /alexm156; pp.111, 144 /jimveilleux; p.113 /mrohana; p.115 /tambogabr; p.118 /AccesscodeHFM; p.121 /vesilvio; pp.122,124 /mammuth; pp.130, 131 /typo-graphics; p.136 /lissart; p. 139 /dpm75; p.148 /repistu; p.149 /mseidelch; p.150 /sarikkath; p.151 /stevegeer; p.152 /Sound_Of_Silence_87; p.153 /sivarock

Shutterstock.com: p.13 Ajancso; p15 Khirman Vladimir; p.19 Leonardo Viti

Dreamstime.com: p.14 Derek Abbott; p.33 Natalia Klenova; p.71 Tiziano Casalta; p.85 Alessandro Flore; p.86 Lpd82; p.87 Silvano Audisio; p.105 Cristina Deidda; p.120 Asta Plechaviciute; p. 125 Innes Ferguson; p.145 Mauro Bighin

pp. 20, 133 John Ferro Sims/Alamy/Red Dot; p.21 Adam Eastland/Alamy/Red Dot; p.132 Imagebroker/Alamy/Red Dot; p.112 Dennis Marsico/Corbis/Red Dot

pp. 90, 92, 93, 94, 95 Courtesy of Hotel Cave Bianche

pp. 137, 138 Courtesy of Consorzio Vicenza è - Convention and Visitors Bureau

pp. 41, 103 Bill Hocker

pp. 156, 157, 158 , 159, 160, 161, 164, 165, 166, 167, 168, 169 Hadley Kincade